SWEATER SUCCESS

From Cast-on to Closet, Learn to Fearlessly Knit Pullovers & Cardigans

Knitatude
Chantal Miyagishima

Quarto.com

First Published in 2026 by Quarry Books, an imprint of The Quarto Group,
100 Cummings Center, Suite 265-D, Beverly, MA 01915, USA.
T (978) 282-9590 F (978) 283-2742

EEA Representation, WTS Tax d.o.o.,
Žanova ulica 3, 4000 Kranj, Slovenia.
www.wts-tax.si

Quarry Books titles are also available at discount for retail, wholesale, promotional, and bulk purchase. For details, contact the Special Sales Manager by email at specialsales@quarto.com or by mail at The Quarto Group, Attn: Special Sales Manager, 100 Cummings Center, Suite 265-D, Beverly, MA 01915, USA.

10 9 8 7 6 5 4 3 2 1

ISBN: 978-0-7603-9699-5

Digital edition published in 2026
eISBN: 978-0-7603-9700-8

Library of Congress Cataloging-in-Publication Data is available.

Design and Page Layout: Kelley Galbreath
Photography: Kaela Caron
Illustrations: Pamela Norman Berman

Printed in China

Dedication

To those who look at sweaters in the mall and think, "I could knit that."

Contents

Welcome and Hi!

HELLO MY LOVE,

Welcome to my book. My name is Chantal, and I am the purple-haired, potty-mouth knitter, designer, and owner of Knitatude, a.k.a. knitting with attitude. I am so tickled that you're on your sweater journey and that I get to be a part of it.

I am going to be honest with you: I never expected to design knitwear, let alone knit or design sweaters like the ones you will find in this book. I'm a late bloomer when it comes to the craft world. My grandmother never taught me, my mom didn't knit (except for us as kids), and sports and dance were more of the scene in my household. Though I was always drawn to the arts—hello singing, dancing, and acting—I never picked up a set of needles until I turned 22, . . . with the exception of a very small blip in seventh grade when my friends tried to teach me, and I ended up with more of a triangle than a scarf.

My journey: In 2012, I fell in love with every basic b*tch and their circle scarf on Pinterest, and I thought, "This is it. This is my passion. I am going to knit myself a circle scarf." I also thought this because I was too cheap and couldn't afford to buy one. Whoops! Turns out knitting was much more challenging than I anticipated, much more expensive, and it took me much longer than most knitters to catch on and get the hang of it. For example, if you're struggling with your first sweater, just know that I didn't learn how to purl until a year into my knitting journey. You've already surpassed me, babe. You're doin' great!

Then 2014 hit and I opened up my Etsy shop and started slinging knits at markets and online. As a person who couldn't follow a pattern for the life of me (I swear they read like Klingon), I was always experimenting and making up my own patterns for the items that popped up in my booth. Fast-forward to 2016, and I decided to write those steps down for the first time. This is how I ended up designing my first piece: the Bumhugger.

From there, I was bitten by the design bug, and that led me to want to make my first sweater. But I didn't really know where to start or how to go about it, and there weren't really books that could guide me. *hint hint*

Cause let's be serious: *sweaters are intimidating* (as I am sure you know). They look complicated and can sometimes involve seaming. It can feel like you need to learn a whole new set of skills to make your first one. But truth be told, sweaters are just two rectangles and two triangles that are assembled or three tubes smashed together. If you can knit a square, a triangle, and a hat, I promise that you can knit a sweater. Because really, there is nothing like that feeling when you pop your head through the neck hole, shimmy it down over your shoulders, and tug the hem so you can see it in its final glory in the mirror. It's electrifying. It's such a rush and such a feeling of accomplishment that you will never find elsewhere, and I can't wait for you to have that. So, without further ado, let's start your sweater journey.

Cheers,

Chantal

Knitting Your First Sweater

Let's get you on your sweater-making journey!

Chances are you've knit a few scarves, added a couple of hats to your collection, and even knit a baby blanket for that family member or friend. But now? You want more. You're ready to take on the next challenge, test your skills, and try something new. You're ready-ish to dive into making your first garment . . . but you're a little nervous. That's totally understandable.

There are tons of reasons that can make knitting a sweater, dress, or cardigan intimidating. It's probably because it's *something you've never done before*. Maybe it's the seaming process that is daunting, or you're not quite sure how each piece works together, or it could be that you're worried about how time consuming or how big of an undertaking it is to make a sweater. You're not alone. That's why I'm here.

Making your own garments is really a start-to-finish process that is so rewarding and straight-up pretty nifty. Imagine: Wandering into your local yarn shop and walking down each aisle, letting your hands drift over each skein of yarn, pulling it to your face to test the softness on your cheek, and picking the perfect palette. You head home with a lighter wallet but with a bunch of delicious squishiness, snuggle up on the couch, and cast on. Periodically, you stand in front of your mirror as you try on your pattern and make adjustments tailored for the perfect fit. Before you know it, you're braving the annoying task of weaving in your ends and blocking your

Working Magic

Being able to knit your own garments is seriously the most rewarding experience, and that even doubles in today's age of fast fashion. There's something so incredibly breathtaking about taking the time to slow down and create fabric with the warmth and love of your own two hands. Not to mention that knitting your own garments is a perfect way of creating items that fit *your* body versus the other way round. By being able to adjust and modify our stitch counts and shaping through yarn, we're combating the relentless barrages of the fashion industry while paying homage to the countless people before us who made their own clothes. So, I see you, my little rebel. And I am here to urge you on. There's really something unique about creating every single stitch, and I want you to cherish that because that itself is *magic*. I am so excited that we're embarking on this adventure together. **Let's make your first sweater a success.**

piece before finally stepping out in public to get those "Where did you buy that?!" compliments, to which you excitedly reply, "I made it!" Sounds pretty cool, right?

In this book, we are going to break down all those steps, teaching you the basics so you can make your first sweater a success. By the end of this book, you'll understand different garment constructions and the needed skillset associated with each one; ease and how to pick your size; yarn subbing and how to choose your yarn and needles, while taking into consideration why specific yarns are better for particular projects or seasons and the different qualities and characteristics of each fiber. You'll have learned about gauge swatching and why it's so important when knitting a garment; modifications; how to read a pattern with multiple sizes; and how to block and take care of your finished garment. Each step in this book is broken down for you in the same order as you would be making your item, giving you the perfect blueprint to ensure your first sweater is a hit.

In each chapter, you will find a TLDR at the end—a.k.a. "Too long. Didn't read." This will wrap up everything we learned in the chapter in one tiny paragraph, like a cheat sheet. This makes it easy to skim your way through—because I know we're all pretty busy, and I want to give you all the time to *knit*

ONE

Basic Garment Constructions and Styles

Okay, you're ready to take on your first sweater, but the question is: what *kind* of sweater? When it comes to garment making, there are a few basic constructions and styles that you are going to find over and over in your pattern hunt. The garment constructions we will cover in this book are seamed, seamless, top-down, and bottom-up. The garment styles we will go through are the drop shoulder, the circular yoke, and the raglan. Once you know the differences, they are pretty easy to spot!

Before you click "purchase" on a pattern online, take a quick look to see if it tells you how the garment is constructed and its style. That way, you're set up for success. We are going through the main constructions and styles (and their subcategories) so you know how to work them, how to spot them, and what makes each one tick.

METHODS OF CONSTRUCTION

Seamed vs. Seamless

Aptly named, a seamless sweater has no seams, but a seamed sweater is assembled by sewing parts together. For most beginners, a seamed pullover or cardigan is usually the most approachable garment construction because it's the easiest to visualize and grasp. Essentially, you are taking two squares (the front and back panels) and two rectangles (the sleeves) and seaming them together at the shoulders, torso, and sleeves. So, we will start there.

SEAMED SWEATERS

Let's look at how a seamed drop shoulder sweater is constructed on the next page. If you reference Diagram 1, you'll see that the arrows run along the seams of the sweater and point in the direction you sew them. You can see that the shoulders are seamed with a space for the neck hole, the torso is seamed with gaps for the sleeves, and the sleeves are seamed around the armhole and down the middle of the underarm. Seaming can be done in multiple ways, including the invisible vertical and horizontal seams, mattress stitch, and whip stitch. These are the most common seaming techniques, but there are plenty of fun ones out there.

How to knit a seamed garment: Knit each piece separately and then assemble your sweater together using the seaming technique recommended in the pattern. Yes, you can substitute another seaming method if you prefer.

Advantages of a seamed garment: Seams are supreme. They are *strong*. This means that your garment will keep its shape the best out of all the styles we cover in this chapter.

Disadvantages of a seamed garment: You can't try on your sweater as you knit it. You're pretty much forced to see how it fits once the knitting is finished and it's been assembled. Also, most knitters don't enjoy the seaming process, as it can be a bit tedious. But for the strength in those seams . . . totally worth it!

SEAMLESS SWEATERS

These sweaters are not knit and then sewn together in segments, but instead are worked in ways that eliminate the need to stitch panels together. We will get into more detail about these as we go through some of the garment styles, but the main thing to know is that there is little to no seaming or assembly required for a seamless sweater.

Bottom-Up vs. Top-Down

Sweaters are usually knit in one of two ways: top-down or bottom-up (see Diagram 2). As the names suggest, top-down garments are worked from the neck down to the hem of your garment. Bottom-up sweaters are worked in reverse—the hem up to the neckline. Both methods have you knit the sleeves last. All the styles we will be going through can be knit both ways, but you will most commonly see circular yokes and raglans being knit top-down, while drop shoulders are most often knit bottom-up.

Can you knit a sweater side to side? You sure can. However, it doesn't tend to happen regularly.

Diagram 1: Seamed, drop shoulder sweater before (top) and after (bottom) seaming.

Diagram 2: Sweaters knit from the bottom up (top) start at the hem. Sweaters knit from the top down (bottom) start at the neckline.

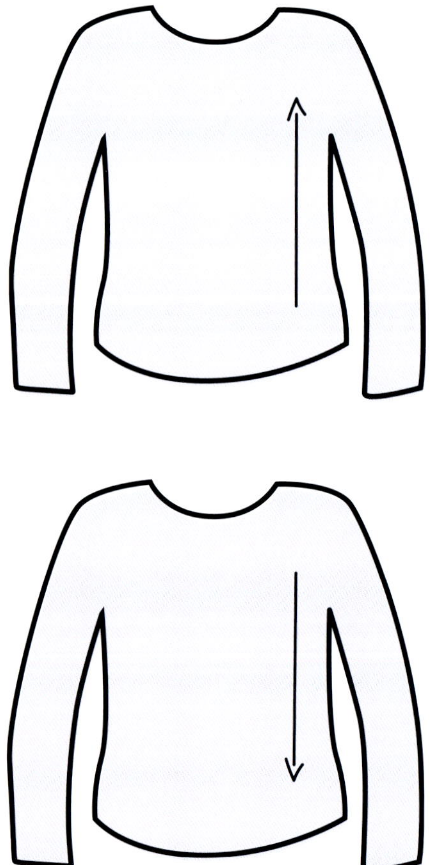

SWEATER STYLES

Just as there are different garment constructions, there are also different garment styles. The names of the styles usually reference something happening in the upper part of the sweater (a.k.a. the yoke, as we call it in knitting). So, as you read about each style, see if you can spot the differences between each one simply by questioning what's happening between the underarm and the neckline.

The Drop Shoulder

This style creates a garment that sounds exactly like its name: a shoulder that drops (see Diagram 3). When this sweater is worn, the shoulder seam—where the sleeve piece meets the body piece—falls just past the natural shoulder line, down your arm. The way this style hangs off the shoulder creates a more relaxed, oversized look. Ease (covered in chapter 3, p. 27) also plays a role in the look and how far down the arm the shoulder drops. The Neapolitan Pullover (p. 94) and Afternoon Tea Cardi (p. 110) are drop shoulder sweaters in this book.

Sometimes you'll see a "modified drop shoulder" with "in-set sleeves." While a regular drop shoulder doesn't have a lot of underarm shaping, a modified drop shoulder has stitches cast-on or bound-off in the armholes at the underarm to create a slightly different shape. An in-set sleeve is worked similarly to the drop shoulder, but goes a bit farther by pushing the sleeve *into* the body of the sweater. Pattern designers tailor the pattern with decreases or increases in the rows between the underarm and shoulder to create a curve in the fabric. This curve eliminates any additional bulky fabric in the underarm.

How to knit a drop shoulder: There are three common ways to knit a drop shoulder sweater. Each option works well, but note that you'll always have a seam at the shoulder of a drop shoulder sweater.

Seamed—You will knit your pieces (front, back, and two sleeves) separately and seam them together.

Top-down—Starting at the neckline, you will knit the front and back panels, join the panels together at the underarm, and knit the body down to the hem. Then, you'll pick up and knit each sleeve from the shoulder to the wrist.

Bottom-up—You will cast on at the hem, work in the round to the underarms, separate for the front and back panels, and then work each panel individually flat. Once you bind off the shoulder (3-needle bind-off or seamed), you will pick up and knit each sleeve from the shoulder to the wrist.

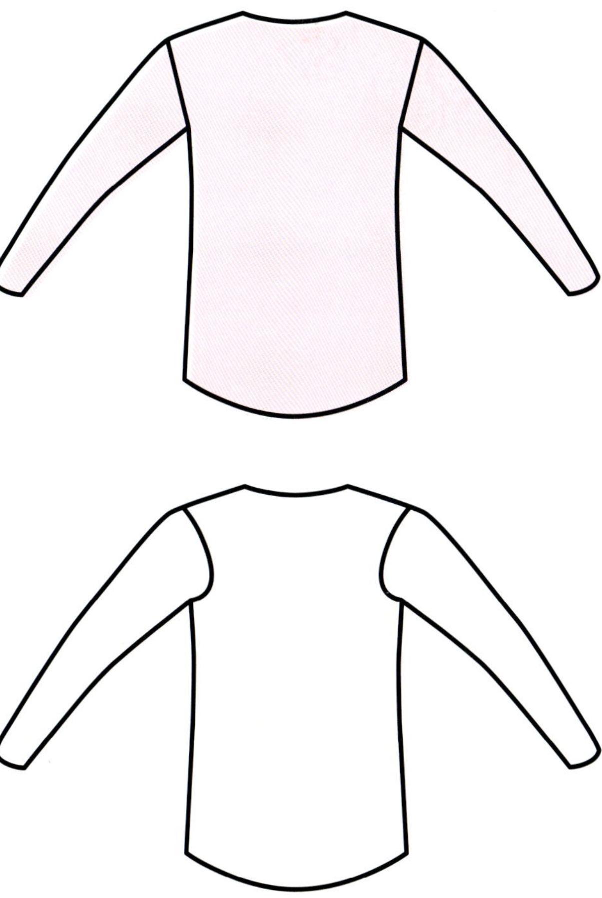

Diagram 3: Drop shoulder–style sweaters (top) have shoulder seams that land on the upper arm rather than the point of the shoulder. Modified drop shoulder sweaters (bottom) have in-set sleeves that remove some of the bulk in fabric at the underarm.

Note Drop shoulders, modified drop shoulders, and raglans can all be seamed or seamless.

Advantages of a drop shoulder: The drop shoulder gives a classic, relaxed look that can easily be tailored for fit through a modified drop shoulder with in-set sleeves. It can be knit with or without seams, meaning you can use circular needles and do away with the pesky task of seaming at the end of your project and try it on as you go, or choose seams for their sturdiness.

Disadvantages of a drop shoulder: To be honest, there isn't much of a disadvantage to a drop shoulder unless you're just not a fan of the style. One thing to note is that a well-designed drop shoulder should always have in-set sleeves for the larger sizes. If your pattern does not have this, you might be left with quite a lot of bulky fabric in the armpits or a shoulder seam near your elbow for the plus sizes. It's usually the first tell of a poorly graded pattern, so just be on the lookout.

THE CIRCULAR YOKE SWEATER

This yoke ain't no joke! Usually knit top-down, this garment style is best known for not having shoulder seams and being a completely seamless sweater. Great for colorwork and lace, this construction essentially radiates from the neckline out with a few increase rows, interspersed with chunks of just plain knitting. The Classic Yoke Sweater (p. 78) is an example of this style.

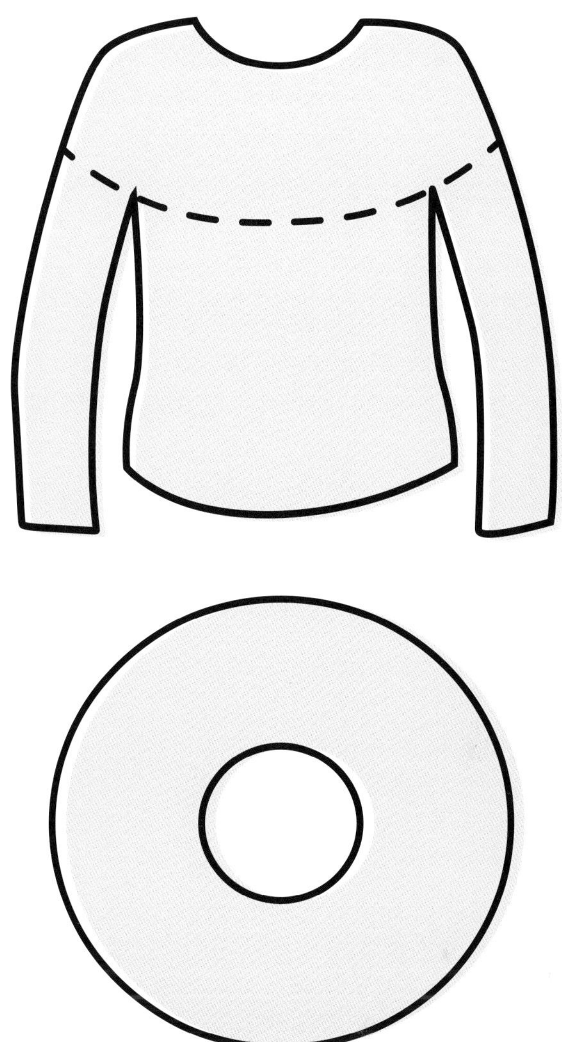

Diagram 4: Sweaters with a circular yoke create a ring of fabric that seamlessly drapes over the shoulders down to the underarm.

In garment making, the yoke describes that area of the upper chest and back that is in between the underarm and neck/shoulders (see Diagram 4). I like to think that it's called a "yoke" because it looks like an egg and its yolk. The yellow egg yolk in the middle is your neck hole, while the fluffy white surrounding it is the fabric that covers your upper chest, back, and shoulders. Is this really why it's called a yoke? Probably not, but it makes it easy to remember! If you lay the yoke section flat, it is essentially a circle (hence "circular") with another circle in the middle (the neck hole).

How to knit a circular yoke: There are two ways you can knit a circular yoke.

Top-down—You will cast on for your neck hole, and in a series of increase rounds, you will quickly increase the number of stitches per round as you work the upper body, shoulders, and sleeves all at once. When you reach the underarm, you will separate the sleeves from the body of the sweater by placing your sleeve stitches "on hold." As you work across the separation row and move sleeve stitches to scrap yarn (using a darning needle, thread waste yarn through the live stitches), you'll cast on stitches in the underarm. The remainder of the body will continue in the round and work toward the hem. Once the body section is finished, you'll put the sleeve stitches that were "on hold" back on your needles to knit from the upper arm to the wrist.

Bottom-up—You will cast on at the hem, working in the round to the underarms. Once finished with the body section, it is set aside while you will work both arms individually from the wrist up to the upper arm. Once your body and two sleeves are ready to be assembled, you will join them all together for the yoke. You will then knit the yoke, and in a series of decrease rounds, you will quickly decrease the number of stitches per round as you work toward the neck hole.

Advantages of a circular yoke: Hello, seamless! Yokes are completely seam-free, meaning you don't have any assembly at the end. (Weaving in your ends and blocking don't count as assembly.) Top-down circular yokes can be tried on as you go, making it easy to adjust length for your torso and arms, or add waist shaping.

Disadvantages of a circular yoke: Sadly, without seams, these sweaters lack of structure and integrity. Meaning, without shoulder seams, this can make for a less durable item that is more prone to growing and stretching with wear.

THE RAGLAN

Much like the circular yoke, the raglan style is essentially a sweater that doesn't have a shoulder seam and is completely seamless. Raglans are mainly known for visually striking diagonal lines that break up the sweater into four quadrants: front, back, and two shoulders. Where the circular yoke increased quickly over just a few rounds, the raglan is much more gradual, with increases usually happening in each quadrant every second round (unless it's a compound raglan, which we'll touch on later)(see Diagram 5). These increases create the classic and telltale "baseball t-shirt" look of the style, which allows for more movement in the shoulders. It is less restrictive than a circular yoke, and that's why baseball players wear them! In this book, there are two raglan designs: the Simple Stockinette Raglan (p. 86) and the Everyday Duster (p. 120).

How to knit a raglan: There are three ways you can knit a raglan.

Diagram 5: When laid flat, the yoke of the raglan creates a rectangular shape as you work its signature diagonal increases.

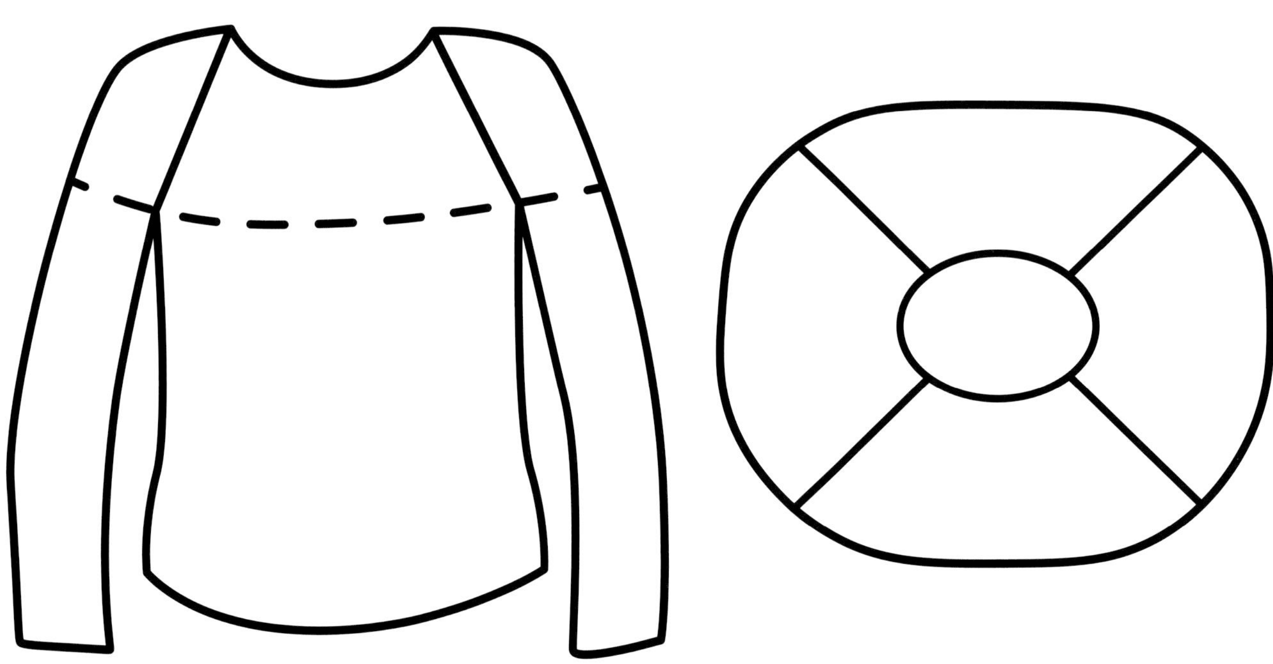

Seamed—You will knit your pieces (front, back, and two sleeves) separately and seam them together.

Top-down—You will cast on for your neck hole and begin increasing stitches on every second round* in four places, making four sections (front, right shoulder, back, and left shoulder). By doing this, you work your upper body, shoulders, and sleeves all at once. When you get to the underarm separation, you will place the stitches for both sleeve sections on hold, casting on stitches in the underarm. The remainder of the body will be joined in the round and worked toward the hem. Once the body section is finished, you will work the sleeves from the upper arm to the wrist.

Bottom-up—You will cast on at the hem, working in the round to the underarms. Once finished with the body section, you will work both arms individually from the wrist up to the upper arm. Once your body and two sleeves are ready to be assembled, you will join them together to knit in the round for the yoke. The four sections (both arms, front, and back) are created by decreasing stitches on every second round* as you work toward the neck hole.

Advantages of a raglan: Raglans are entirely seamless, meaning you don't have any assembly to do at the end. (Remember, weaving in your ends and blocking don't count as assembly.) Top-down raglans are great, as you can try them on as you go, making it easy to adjust the length for your torso and arms and add waist shaping and short rows.

Disadvantages of a raglan: Like any garment without seams, sadly this has a lack of structure and integrity. Without shoulder seams, this can make for a less durable item that is more prone to growing and stretching with wear.

*This is a generalization about the rate of increase. Some designers may change this to modify the shape slightly for a particular stitch pattern. Or, they may modify it heavily to create a "compound" raglan, which changes the shape to reduce bulky fabric gathering at the underarm.

This information scratches the surface on the many ways to construct sweaters and the styles that are out there. We didn't even get into all the shapes the body can take on (straight, A-line, and tapered, oh my!). What you have here, though, is the basics to get you started. All the rest will come with time. And hey, now that you know more about how garments are constructed and the various styles you can knit, grab a few sweaters from your closet. Can you tell if they're seamed or seamless? Do you have a raglan, circular yoke, or drop shoulder in your wardrobe? Grab your favorite and keep it handy; it will be helpful to have as a reference when reading future chapters on ease and fit

TLDR-
Too long. Didn't read.

When it comes to garment styles, there are a few main types: drop shoulder, circular yoke, and raglan. Each one has signature details that make them easy to tell apart. Drop shoulders have shoulder seams that tend to *drop off* the top of your shoulder, landing further down the upper arm. Circular yokes and raglans don't have shoulder seams and are most often seamless. Raglans are easy to spot with their four sharp diagonal lines that run from the neckline to the underarms.

A garment can be constructed many ways: seamed, seamless, top-down, and bottom-up. Each method has its own pros and cons and can be done on any of the garment styles. It really comes down to the designer's preference and style, and which method *you* like best.

TWO

Finding Your Size

Armed with an understanding of the style of sweater you want to knit and how it is constructed, it's time to figure out what size you'll be knitting. You might be wondering, "why do I have to measure my body?" I know you've been buying clothes for years and you know what size to grab off the rack. You have probably noticed by now that there are a lot of variations in sizes store to store. Generally, you're okay grabbing the same size, but sometimes the sleeves are too long or the hem is too cropped. Right?

Knitting your own sweaters means you have the chance to get just the fit you want, but you need to start somewhere. We need the baseline to know which of the sizes planned in a pattern will get you what you're looking for. Just like retail stores, even though most designers work off sizing standards, you're going to find a lot of variations from designer to designer. Taking your measurements will take the guessing game out of choosing a size.

In the future, you might want to knit a sweater for a friend or family member (lucky them!). If you can't measure them (perhaps because it's a gift), you can use the standards we talk about in this chapter to help choose a size. So keep that in mind too as you read about sizing.

You Are Fabulous as You Are

Before we start this chapter, I want to give you some love. Measuring yourself is not for the faint of heart. With the fashion industry and society always pushing us to feel bad about ourselves because of a number or a letter, it is *hard* not to see these numbers and have mixed emotions. However, I want you to know that those numbers . . . they are *only* numbers. And by knowing them (instead of guessing), you can make a sweater that fits and that you'll feel amazing in. I promise that knowing your measurements only makes for a great sweater, not something negative. So, if you have any negative thoughts, I want you to dropkick them into oblivion. We're not into that negative self-talk here, and I won't allow you to do it to yourself!

TAKING MEASUREMENTS

When designers plan their garments, the bust/chest circumference is the measurement most often used to distinguish sizes. But there are a few other measurements that we want to peek at and jot down for later, just in case we want to make any modifications (which we'll talk about in a later chapter, see p. 61). Those are the waist, hip, upper arm, and underarm-to-wrist length. Let's start with how to properly measure each of these. All you need is a fabric tape measure, pencil, and place to write your measurements.

To make things easier, I've created a simple croquis for you to log your measurements. Scan the provided QR code with your smartphone or visit www.quarto.com/files/SweaterSuccess to download and print the body croquis. FYI, croquis is a fashion term for a rough draft or sketch. In this case, that sketch is the outline of a body showing you the various places we'll measure.

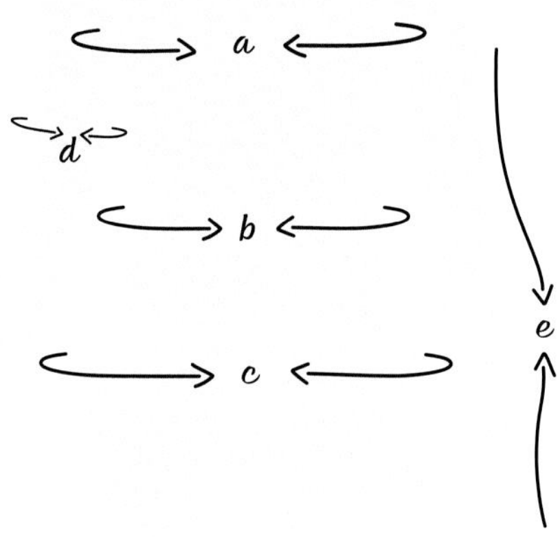

How to Measure Your Bust (A)

Wrap the tape measure loosely around the fullest part of your chest, about nip height. Note your measurement in inches and centimeters. When measuring, make sure you don't push out all the air and don't take in a big breath. You'll want to take your measurement while your bust/chest is at its resting state. If you wear a bra, make sure to do this with your everyday bra, as this is what you'll be wearing under your garment.

How Often Should I Measure My Body?

Taking body measurements isn't a once-and-done task, sorry to say. Our bodies change all the time, so it's a good idea to do a quick check of at least your bust/chest measurement before you start a new sweater. You're about to put in a significant chunk of time to make a sweater, you want it to fit when you're done.

How to Measure Your Waist (B)

Next, loosely measure around the smallest section of your torso; this is typically level with your belly button. Again, note your measurement in inches and centimeters. When measuring, make sure you don't hold your breath, suck in your stomach, or breathe out too much. You want to take the measurement right after you exhale.

How to Measure Your Hips (C)

Standing with your feet together, measure your hips by loosely wrapping the tape at the widest part of your rear. Note your measurement in inches and centimeters.

How to Measure Your Upper Arm (D)

Standing up straight and with your arm relaxed at your side, wrap your fabric measuring tape around the middle of your upper arm at the midpoint between your shoulder and elbow. The tape should be a bit snug but not so tight that it feels like it's pinching. Note your measurement in inches and centimeters.

How to Measure Your Underarm to Your Wrist (E)

This one is a bit tricky to do one-handed, so it may be helpful to ask a friend. Using a fabric measuring tape, lift your arm until it is horizontal with your shoulders. Relax your neck and shoulder and let your arm slightly bend. Measure from your armpit to your wrist. Note your measurement in inches and centimeters.

SIZING STANDARDS

Now that you know your measurements, let's find your size. One thing to know is that designers base their patterns on standardized sizes, such as those created by the Craft Yarn Council. These numbers are based on averages—for simplicity, they've been sorted into ranges. Don't worry if you aren't standard! No one is. We are all unique.

To determine your size, you will want to match your bust/chest measurement with the "standard size." Remember, the letters and numbers aren't a representation of you. We're just looking for the garment dimensions that will fit you the way you want them to fit.

Standard Bust/Chest Sizes

XS: 28–30" (71–76 cm)
S: 32–34" (81–86 cm)
M: 36–38" (91–97 cm)
L: 40–42" (102–107 cm)
XL: 44–46" (112–117 cm)
2X: 48–50" (122–127 cm)
3X: 52–54" (132–137 cm)
4X: 56–58" (142–147 cm)
5X: 60–62" (152–158 cm)

You'll notice that sizes jump by 4" (10 cm), but there is a 2" (5 cm) gap between sizes. Don't worry. If you have a bust/chest size that is in between sizes, you get more control over your ease. You can choose to size down for a snugger fit or size up for a baggier fit.

Other Standardized Sizes

Since the patterns in this book are based on the Craft Yarn Council women's standards, it is helpful to know the sizes for other areas of the body, too. Table 1 (at 24) includes

Table 1

Standardize sizing set by the Craft Yarn Council. Source: Craft Yarn Council's www.YarnStandards.com

	XS	S	M	L	XL	2X	3X	4X	5X
Chest (A)	28–30" (71–76 cm)	32–34" (81–86 cm)	36–38" (91.5–96.5 cm)	40–42" (101.5–106.5 cm)	44–46" (111.5–117 cm)	48–50" (122–127 cm)	52–54" (132–137 cm)	56–58" (142–147 cm)	60–62" (152–158 cm)
Center Back Neck-to-Wrist	26–26½" (66–68.5 cm)	27–27½" (68.5–70 cm)	28–28½" (71–72.5 cm)	29–29½" (73.5–75 cm)	29–29½" (73.5–75 cm)	30–30½" (76.5–77.5 cm)	30½ –31" (77.5–79 cm)	31½–32" (80–81.5 cm)	31½–32" (80–81.5 cm)
Back-to-Waist Length	16½" (42 cm)	17" (43 cm)	17¼" (43.5 cm)	17½" (44.5 cm)	17¾" (45 cm)	18" (45.5 cm)	18" (45.5 cm)	18½" (47 cm)	18½" (47 cm)
Crossback (shoulder to shoulder)	14–14½" (35.5–37 cm)	14½–15" (37–38 cm)	15½–16" (39.5–40.5 cm)	16½–17" (42–43 cm)	17½" (44.5 cm)	18" (45.5 cm)	18" (45.5 cm)	18½" (47 cm)	18½" (47 cm)
Arm Length to Wrist (E)	16½" (42 cm)	17" (43 cm)	17" (43 cm)	17½" (44.5 cm)	17½" (44.5 cm)	18" (45.5 cm)	18" (45.5 cm)	18½" (47 cm)	18½" (47 cm)
Upper Arm (D)	9¾" (25 cm)	10¼" (26 cm)	11" (28 cm)	12" (30.5 cm)	18½" (34.5 cm)	18½" (39.5 cm)	17" (43 cm)	18½" (47 cm)	18½" (49.5 cm)
Armhole Depth	6–6½" (15.5–16.5 cm)	6½–7" (16.5–17.5 cm)	7–7½" (17.5–19 cm)	7½–8" (19–20.5 cm)	8–8½" (20.5–21.5 cm)	8½–9" (21.5–23 cm)	9–9½" (23–24 cm)	9½–10" (24–25.5 cm)	10–10½" (25.5–26.5 cm)
Waist (B)	23–24" (58.5–61 cm)	25–26½" (63.5–67.5 cm)	28–30" (71–76 cm)	32–34" (81.5–86.5 cm)	36–38" (91.5–96.5 cm)	40–42" (101.5–106.5 cm)	44–45" (111.5–114 cm)	46–47" (116.5–119 cm)	49–50" (124–127 cm)
Hips (C)	33–34" (83.5–86 cm)	35–36" (89–91.5 cm)	38–40" (96.5–101.5 cm)	42–44" (106.5–111.5 cm)	46–48" (116.5–122 cm)	52–53" (132–134.5 cm)	54–55" (137–139.5 cm)	56–57" (142–144.5 cm)	61–62" (155–157 cm)

those measurements. The chart represents actual body measurements, not the finished garment measurements.

Even though it's not necessary to take all these measurements on your body, you can! For example, ask a friend to measure your shoulders across your upper back. If you want a perfectly tailored top with a crisp fit in the shoulders, you can see where that measurement falls on the table under "Crossback." Knowing this will give you a good idea if the finished garment will be fitted in the shoulders or not. Same goes for the other measurements.

As you knit more and more sweaters and learn to modify patterns (p. 61) to suit your needs, all these details come into play. For example, my bust measurement is 36½" (92.5 cm), which lands me in the M size range on Table 1. However, my upper arm circumference is 12" (30 cm) instead of 11" (28 cm). This puts my upper arms in the L size range. This means I can choose to make some modifications in the pattern to accommodate a better fit for me down the road.

TLDR-Too long. Didn't read.

More often than not, your pullover or cardigan pattern size is determined by your bust/chest circumference. Pattern designers use "standardized sizing," but nobody is "standard," so measuring is a must.

To take your measurements, you will need a fabric tape measure and yourself (or the person you will be making the item for if gifting a sweater). Measure the following:

- Bust/chest circumference
- Waist circumference
- Hip circumference
- Upper arm circumference
- Under-arm-to-wrist length

The "standards" for these measurements inform the size ranges that designers use. Find where you fall in these ranges and start with that size.

Standard Bust/Chest Sizes

XS: 28–30" (71–76 cm)
S: 32–34" (81–86 cm)
M: 36–38" (91–97 cm)
L: 40–42" (102–107 cm)
XL: 44–46" (112–117 cm)
2X: 48–50" (122–127 cm)
3X: 52–54" (132–137 cm)
4X: 56–58" (142–147 cm)
5X: 60–62" (152–158 cm)

Note: These sizes are *not* the finished garment sizes.

While a bit daunting to do, taking your measurements is helpful in case you might want to make modifications. Using these standardized sizes is a great way to see where you might want to alter the pattern to create a more personalized fit. Next, we'll talk about ease, which is the difference between your body size and the sweater's measurements.

FUJINON ASPHERICAL LENS

THREE

Easing into Ease

Now that you know your measurements, it's time to talk about ease. Ease can be a bit tricky to wrap your head around, but I promise it's simply about how tight-fitting or baggy the garment will be on your body.

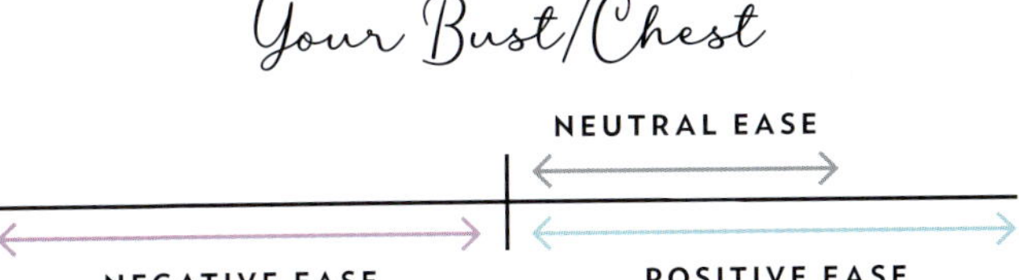

WHAT IS EASE?

By industry standards, ease is the difference between your physical body measurement and the finished garment. Most designers will let you know how much ease is suggested based on their knitted sample, or you'll find sentences like "designed to be worn with 4–6" (10–15 cm) of positive ease in mind" in their pattern notes. This essentially lets us know how close or far away the garment will measure from the bust/chest—because ease is determined by the bust/chest measurement.

WHAT TYPES OF EASE ARE THERE?

In the knitting and crochet world, you will hear three main terms: negative ease, neutral ease, and positive ease. There are subsets in these categories, too. Before we delve in too deep, let's run through those first over-arching three first.

Negative Ease—Negative ease is when the garment dimensions are smaller than your bust/chest measurement. This makes the garment tighter and gives a more form-hugging fit. Ever put on a shirt or sweater, and it felt like it was pulling in? That's negative ease! Technically, anything that dips below 0" (0 cm) from your own bust/chest measurement is in the negative range.

Neutral Ease—Neutral ease is when the garment dimensions are either the exact same as your bust/chest circumference or a couple of inches or centimeters more. If you've ever put on a shirt or sweater and it fit a little looser than your bust/chest but didn't feel too oversized, chances are it has neutral ease. This is the most common type of ease you will find when going on your pattern search, but it does dip into the "positive ease area" a wee bit.

Positive Ease—Positive ease is when the garment dimensions are bigger than your bust/chest circumference. Ever put on a super oversized sweater and snuggled up in its roomy warmth? That, my friend, is positive ease. Note that, technically, positive ease

The Simple Stockinette Raglan (p. 86) is shown with ½" (1.3 cm) of negative ease.

encapsulates neutral ease as well since it's on the positive side of the scale, but do know that the overall sentiment is that positive ease results in an oversized, baggy-type fit.

Overall, designers will play with ease to create different silhouettes, amp up the cozy and comfy vibes, or create distinct fashion styles and aesthetics to fit trends.

WHAT ARE THE STANDARD FITS?

Outside of the three main categories of negative, neutral, and positive ease, there are different subsets that start to branch off into a bit more detail. Just know that they essentially range on the scale from neutral to positive ease, constantly revolving around the bust/chest circumference.

How Fits Are Described

Very Close Fit = 2–4" (5–10 cm) of negative ease
Close fit = 1–2" (2–5 cm) of positive ease
Standard/classic fit = 2–4" (5–10 cm) of positive ease
Loose fit = 4–6" (10–15 cm) of positive ease
Oversized fit = 6+" (15+ cm) of positive ease

IS EASE DESIGNED INTO THE PATTERN OR DO I NEED TO FIGURE IT OUT MYSELF?

The answer is: It can be both. Most (if not all) designers are basing their garments on standardized sizes like those

The Classic Yoke Sweater (p. 78) is shown with 3½" (9 cm) of neutral ease.

The Neapolitan Sweater (p. 94) is shown with 6½" (16.5 cm) of positive ease.

set by the Craft Yarn Council. It just depends on how they word the essential fit information in their patterns.

All my patterns have the intended ease designed into the garment. This means that I will give you the standardized measurements up front, and all you need to do is measure yourself, match it up, and knit the size that is according to it.

These sizes are designed to fit a bust/chest measurement of:
XS fits 28–30" (71–76 cm) bust/chest
S fits 32–34" (81–86 cm) bust/chest
M fits 36–38" (91–97 cm) bust/chest
L fits 40–42" (101–107 cm) bust/chest
XL fits 44–46" (112–117 cm) bust/chest
2X fits 48–50" (122–127 cm) bust/chest
3X fits 52–54" (132–137 cm) bust/chest
4X fits 56–58" (142–147 cm) bust/chest
5X fits 60–62" (154–157 cm) bust/chest

In other words, if your bust/chest measures 42" (107 cm), you would knit the size large (based on the sizes seen here) to get the same ease as is seen in the sample size. Tada! However, if the designer says something like "designed to be worn with 4–6" (10–15 cm) of positive ease," you should check the finished bust/chest measurements in the pattern and see what size is 4–6" (10–15 cm) larger than your own bust/chest measurement.

CAN I PICK MY OWN EASE?

Heck yes, you can! If you find a pattern that you love but aren't totally tickled with the ease that is suggested or knit in the sample, you can play around and mix and match sizes. Simply put, knit a size that has the ease you want. For example: Do you like something a bit baggier than the pattern? Bump up a size. Do you want something that's tighter fitting? Feel free to bump down a size or two. The main thing is to do what makes you comfortable.

Not sure what ease you personally like? Head to your closet and pick out your favorite sweater. Give it a measure across the chest while it's lying flat. Double that number, and you've got the bust/chest circumference of that sweater. Compare it to your own bust/chest measurement and do the light math to figure out how many inches or centimeters of ease it is. Then knit the size that has the finished measurements and ease that you like.

TLDR-Too long. Didn't read.

Ease comes down to how form-fitting or baggy a garment will fit. Ease itself is determined by the difference between your physical body measurement (mainly based on the bust or chest circumference) and the finished garment measurement. By industry standards, ease is broken down into three categories: negative, neutral, and positive ease. Negative ease means tighter fit; neutral ease means slightly larger than your own bust/chest; and positive means baggy or oversized. When looking for patterns, some designers have the intended ease already designed in, which is based on standardized sizing, while others have suggestions of what ease you want to knit based on their finished sample. You are free to play around with whatever ease you like, or you can knit the size according to the designer's instructions. It's up to you!

LANTERN MOON

FOUR

Essential Sweater Tools

You've picked your size in the pattern you're going to knit and it's going to have the right amount of ease for you. Huzzah! It's time to scrounge up all the materials you'll need to be able to complete your garment. In every pattern, you will find a list of recommended tools and materials, which will include the needle size, yarn weight and yardage/meterage, and the miscellaneous tools you will need to complete the pattern. This chapter covers the stuff you're going to use in almost every single pattern to knit time and time again—a.k.a. the tools.

THE BASICS

In every knitter's arsenal, there should be a few standard things. I promise you will use them *all the time,* so it's worthwhile having them on hand and within arm's reach while you knit.

Scissors—Nice, sharp scissors will make changing skeins a breeze.

Measuring tape—A good measuring tape is key for measuring your gauge, your own measurements, and for tracking your way through your pattern.

Darning needle or yarn needle—You'll need one of these to weave in ends as you go or at the end, or for seaming your pieces together.

Stitch markers—Use these handy items to mark your place, be a visual aid for your increases and decreases, track your sections as you knit, or show where your beginning of row/round is

NEEDLES

Obviously, you're going to need some needles! Depending on the way the garment is constructed, you may see callouts for either circular, straight, or double-pointed needles. Let's talk about what these terms mean.

Straight needles—As the name implies, these needles are literally straight, rigid, and usually about 14" (35.5 cm) long. They have a "stopper" on one end that keeps the stitches from sliding off. You will most often see seamed garments knit on these. However, they aren't the best for sweater-making simply because of the number of stitches you will have on one needle at once, especially for the plus sizes.

Double-pointed needles (DNPs)—These are straight like straight needles and rigid, but much shorter and they do not have stoppers on the ends. They have a tip or point at each end. You'll see them sold in sets of four or five. DPNs are used for knitting smaller circumferences in the round, such as necklines or sleeves.

Circular needles (circ)—If you've seen knitting needles with a flexible cable between the rigid needles on each end, those are called circular needles. These come in a range of lengths determined by the cord in between the two needle tips. These are great for sweater knitting, whether seamed or seamless! Depending on what section of the sweater you're working on, you might need 16" (40 cm) needles at the neckline and 24–40" (61–102 cm) needles for the body. The pattern will guide you. Sometimes, you'll see longer lengths required for sleeves if using the "magic loop" method of small-circumference knitting. Essentially, you will want to find the lengths that correspond to what is called for in the pattern. The cables themselves can be plastic or metal.

Metal vs. Plastic vs. Wood

When it comes to picking the material of which the needles are made, it's totally up to you. You can choose between metal, plastic, wood, or a combination. It's all up to personal preference. When you're starting out, you can buy different needle types (or borrow them from a knitting friend) to test them out. Each needle material has pros and cons.

Metal—Metal needles are great for tighter knitters because the yarn slips more easily. They're also loved by lace knitters; their sharp points make decreases effortless. Some people don't care for the click of the metal, and beginners might be frustrated by how slippery they are.

Plastic—Plastic needles can feel nice and smooth in the hand while also holding the stitches well. The plastic shafts have a bit more grip than metal, so they're not as slippery.

Wood—Wood needles are wonderful for looser knitters as they tend to be grippier on the yarn. Beware though, softer wood needles like bamboo can develop dents and grooves over time, which become annoying as knit. Hardwood needles don't have the same wear-and-tear issues.

Synthetic and combination—Many needle manufacturers are using synthetic materials like carbon fibers to create long-lasting, durable needles. Like wood needles, they're grippier and hold the stitches well, without the issue of dents and dings. You may also see needles that have a shaft in one material and tip in another material. These give you the super pointy tip that works well for lace while also having the grip of wood or synthetic materials.

Again, what your needles are made of really depends on your personal preference, so what you choose depends on what you like best!

Interchangeable Sets (1)

If you're planning on getting more into garment making and see more sweaters and cardigans on your horizon, I would suggest investing in an interchangeable needle set. They are more costly upfront, but I promise they will save

Tip My favorite interchangeable set is the LYKKE Crafts Blush set. They have multiple bendy swivel cords, a great range of needle sizes, and are made of a nice wood that isn't too grippy or slippery. Plus, they're pink.

you money and time down the road. For example, if your gauge isn't working out on the first try, you don't have to order another size needle. Simply go up or down to a different needle tip size in the interchangeable set and then you're ready to gauge swatch again without having to go out to buy yet another fixed needle.

STITCH MARKERS

Though I could have left you high and dry without any further info on the stitch markers mentioned in The Basics, I would like to note that all stitch markers are not created equal. There are two types of stitch markers: ring (or closed) stitch markers and locking stitch markers. Both are great to have on hand while creating your first garment.

Ring stitch markers (2)—These closed stitch markers are for marking the beginning of your row and separating sections in your patterns. They stay nicely on your needles without the worry of them falling off mid-row. These will travel with your work as you slip them from the left to the right needle as you knit. Take care not to knit them *into* your project though. They aren't easily removed if you accidentally work them into a stitch.

Locking stitch markers (3)—These markers are not a closed loop—they have a locking feature that allows you to add them to your work at a moment's notice. They are perfect for double-checking row counts, separating stitch repeats across the row (such as lace and cables), and holding onto live stitches (such as the middle stitch of a V-neck while you work the rest of the panels). The clip or lock can pop open from time to time as you work and might fall off. If that happens, you can simply pop it back in place.

The key difference between these two types of markers is the locking feature. Want to easily count your rows? Add a locking stitch marker on the worked piece and continue to knit. When you're done, simply unlock the stitch marker and take it off your piece. Having trouble telling the right side from the wrong side of sweater pieces? Put a locking marker on the front and remove it when it's time to seam the pieces together. See? So useful.

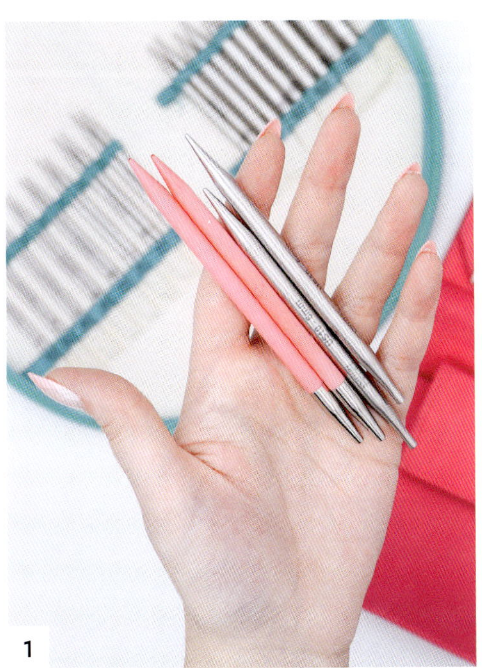
1

2

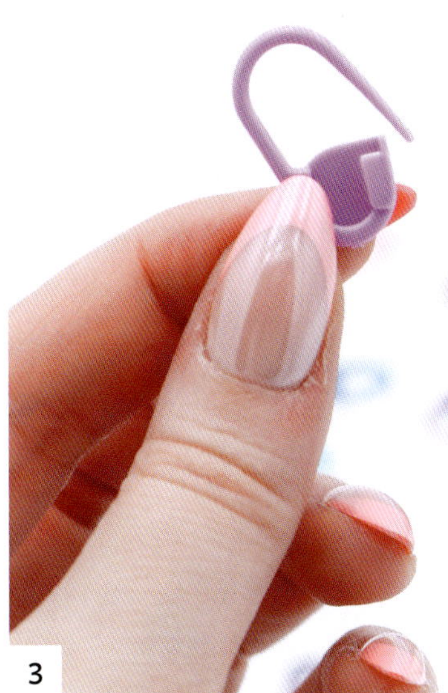
3

BLOCKING TOOLS

If you've been knitting for any length of time, you've probably heard the term "blocking." We will get into what blocking is and how to do it in chapter 9 (p. 67), but here I want to share some handy tools to have at the ready.

Blocking pins—You should already know what a pin is. It's super sharp metal that can tack things in place. Blocking pins do the same thing; they help keep your item in place as you block it out to the correct dimensions. You can purchase blocking pins in the form of a "comb," which has several pins connected together in a straight line, or you can use basic sewing pins. Be sure to choose pins that will not rust because the metal will be next to moisture when you block.

Blocking mats—You'll want to have something to pin your project to when you block it; mats are the answer. They're soft and made of cork or foam. Many look like large puzzle pieces. These allow you to change the shape of the mat to the shape of your project. Not only are they a great flat surface that you won't be afraid to stick blocking pins into, but also the lightweight foam plastic can help speed up drying time.

Absorbent towels—Regular cotton bath towels come in handy when blocking. You'll use them to soak up some of the water before pinning the project out to dry.

Steamers, spray bottles, and water basins—Depending on how you plan to block your piece, you will need one or more of these items to be able to block your garment with water. More details can be found in the blocking chapter (p. 67).

Nonrinse wool wash—When working with wool, it's good to have a quality wool wash on hand to add to your soaking water. Most are nonrinse, so you don't need to worry about running the project through the water again after blocking.

Small fan—Under the category "nice to have" is a small fan. To speed up the drying process, you can point a fan at your project to circulate the air. It can help a project dry in a few hours rather than a few days.

PROJECT BAGS

Keeping your sweater yarn, pieces, tools, and pattern together in one spot is very convenient. So, you'll want to have a project bag for storage (or a pretty basket . . . *something*). Project bags come in a range of sizes and can be handmade from makers on Etsy or something commercially made that you pick up at your local yarn store. It doesn't need to be anything fancy though; you could even store things in a reusable grocery tote! Whatever you use, you won't regret keeping it all together.

TLDR- Too long. Didn't read.

Picking your tools and materials is half the fun of knitting up your project. When getting ready to knit a garment, every knitter should have some basics on hand. Those are scissors, a measuring tape, darning needles, and stitch markers.

Needles: From circular needles to straight needles to double-pointed needles, the needles you'll need to use throughout each pattern's garment construction will usually be dictated by the pattern itself. You are welcome to pick from metal, plastic, or wood and it all comes down to personal preference. If you see a lot of garment knitting in your future, you might want to consider investing in an interchangeable needle set.

Stitch markers: There are two types of stitch markers and they both can play different roles in your knitting. Ring stitch markers are great for tracking where you are and separating stitch counts, while locking stitch markers are wonderful for being able to take on and off in the middle of a row or for placing on any stitch you like as you work your piece.

Blocking materials: Blocking is the last and final step of your sweater journey, and you'll need a few things. Blocking pins and mats are both helpful when pinning out your piece to the right dimensions and shape. Depending on how you'll be blocking your garment, you may need a steamer, a water basin, or a spray bottle. All three of these require water.

FIVE

Yarn and Yarn Subbing

Your needles are prepped and you have all the materials you need . . . now comes the fun part: picking your yarn. Yay! With so many different weights, fibers, and colors to choose from, it can be as exhilarating as it can be overwhelming.

Before we get into the (k)nitty gritty, you'll want to know that when a designer is creating a pattern, they'll have a few things in mind as they select their yarn: drape, structural integrity, fiber content, season, and the overall aesthetic, just to name a few. So, as you're picking your yarn for your finished piece, after reading the info on the next few pages, try to imagine what the designer had in mind. For example, head to page 140 to see why I chose the yarns I did for the patterns in this book. Though, as much as you want to be in the designer's head, you must do what's best for *you*. Multiple deciding factors may influence whether you choose a similar yarn to make it as close to the designer sample or stray from the pattern itself.

WHEN EVERYTHING ALIGNS

If you have access to the yarn called for in the pattern, it's in your budget, and it's the type of fiber you like, that's great! You get the easy job of ordering it and knitting the pattern as it goes. *Claps all around.*

However, if you don't have access to this yarn, whether that's because it's not available in your region, it's been discontinued, you have yarn in your stash you want to use up, you have an allergy to the yarn called for, or you simply don't like it and want a totally different look, you get the fun task of substituting the yarn with another.

HELLO, YARN SUBBING

Yarn subbing is the fondly known short form of "yarn substituting." This is the act of substituting another yarn for the one called for in the pattern. It can be a bit daunting, and it's one of the first steps that can deter a maker from starting their first garment.

I'm here to help make yarn subbing easier. With the information I share here, you'll be able to sub with confidence. We're going to look at the weight classification of the yarn, the yardage (meterage), fiber content, and the type of project when we want to switch things up. Let's go through each one.

YARN WEIGHT

Whenever substituting, you want to pick the same yarn weight for your project as is used in the pattern. This can be laid out in a few different ways. Depending on where they are from, the designer can call out the thickness of yarn by number (#4) or name (worsted). In Europe, you'll sometimes see yarn referred to by the number of plies (4-ply jumper weight). For our purposes, we're going to assume the pattern states either the number or name based on Craft Yarn Council standards.

The most important thing is that you have to match weights. Ball bands are very helpful with this. Grab any nearby skein of yarn and look at the information on the printed label. You should find information that relates to Table 1. When subbing one yarn for another, you want to get details as close as possible. When your skein says it is a #5 and the pattern calls for "Chunky" yarn, you have a match. Better yet, look at the recommended gauges. Does the recommended gauge for the yarn you're looking at match the gauge for the yarn in the pattern?

Breaking Down the Weight Classes

Even though your pattern may call for a #4 yarn, there are subcategories in each weight class. For example, a worsted weight is slightly thinner than an aran weight, but both fall into the #4 class. So, how would you know which one to use if you want to substitute one #4 for another? It's time to pull out our trusty, dusty calculators.

Say you've found yarn in the same weight class; let's check if they are similar in thickness. The way we do this is by calculating the yards (meters) per ounce (gram). We'll work through an example.

Example 1: Your pattern calls for a size #4 yarn and you have a worsted-weight yarn in your stash that you want to use. You look at the ball band and see that your yarn has 155 yards (141.7 meters) per 3½ ounces (100 grams). The yarn used in the patterns states that it has 165 yards (151 meters) per 3½ ounces (100 grams). The yardage by weight here is pretty darn close at just 10 yards (9 meters) difference. This *should* sub well. A good rule of thumb is to stay within a plus or minus 20% range of the original yardage.

Example 2: You also have a sweater quantity of another yarn you're considering for the pattern. This yarn has 125 yards (114.3 meters) per 3½ ounces (100 grams). Compared to the designer's sample that's knit with a yarn that has 165 yards (151 meters) per 3½ ounces (100 grams), that's a 40-yard difference. That might not work as well as the first one you debated on using.

In either example, I suggest knitting a gauge swatch to see if your yarn choice will work. *It's the best way to determine if a yarn is going to substitute well.* If you don't have that exact yarn on hand and your gauge doesn't match the pattern's gauge, it's time to keep shopping.

Can I Sub a Totally Different Yarn Weight?

No. While technically you *can* yarn sub with a different weight, as a designer I am going to strongly point you toward no. Subbing a different yarn weight (for example a #3 when the pattern calls for a #4) will 99.9% of the time result in you being unable to attain gauge, which we will talk about more in the next chapter. Choosing a different yarn weight and not getting gauge will require you to redo the math (stitch counts) in your pattern. I do not recommend this. It's much easier for you to work with the suggested weight yarn than to have to rewrite the entire pattern yourself. Keep that other yarn in your stash for the perfect future project.

Please also note that most designers (including myself) do not help with pattern support questions such as this. But if you're ready to take on that challenge by yourself, that's great. Just know that you're taking a gamble and please do not fault the designer if it doesn't work out. #IHaveHorrorStories

Table 2.

Source: Craft Yarn Council, www.yarnstandards.com

Yarn by Symbol	Yarn by Number	Yarn by Name	Yarn Gauge Range in Stockinette Stitch Over 4" (10 cm)
0 LACE	0	Lace, Cobweb, Light Fingering, Thread	33–40* sts
1 SUPER FINE	1	Super Fine, Sock, Fingering, Baby	27–32 sts
2 FINE	2	Fine, Sport, Baby	23–26 sts
3 LIGHT	3	Light, DK, Light Worsted	21–24 sts
4 MEDIUM	4	Medium, Worsted, Heavy Worsted, Afghan, Aran	16–20 sts
5 BULKY	5	Bulky, Chunky, Craft, Rug	12–15 sts
6 SUPER BULKY	6	Super Bulky, Roving	7–11 sts
7 JUMBO	7	Jumbo, Roving	6 sts and fewer

In some countries, you'll see yarn weights communicated in plies. For example, you might see a "2-ply jumper weight" yarn. Unfortunately, ply isn't a reliable way to measure weight or the thickness of yarn, especially when you think about unique chainette spun yarns. You could have a single-ply fingering weight yarn or a single-ply bulky yarn. Swatching for gauge (p. 47) is really the best way to know if the yarn you want to use will work for your project.

FIBER CONTENTS

Whether the pattern indicates wool, acrylic, cotton, alpaca, or something else, chances are the designer chose a particular fiber content for a reason. Things like drape, season, stretchiness, or structure are all part of the decision-making process. As you are yarn subbing, this will be something you want to pay attention to. This portion of the chapter is going to get pretty nerdy while we get deep into each fiber's characteristics, so buckle up. I promise that knowing all of this fiber information will make it easier in your future decisions of what and what not to yarn sub with for certain projects.

Wool

The one main thing to know about wool is that it holds its shape well because of the lengths and the crimps in its fibers. The fibers interlock together, creating a strong hold on your stitches, and in doing so, keeps them in place. This characteristic alone makes wool perfect for raglan and circular yoke designs. Because there are no shoulder seams in those types of garments, wool can act as an interlocking shield, putting each stitch into place like a battle squad and helping combat the pull of gravity. Wool is also well known for its warmth, so you will usually see it pop up in items that are made for cooler temperatures and colder seasons. However, don't feel like you must always shy away from using wool in warmer climates. Wool has moisture-wicking properties that can help regulate heat, just not as well as cotton does, for example. Aesthetics-wise, some designers will use certain wools for their look alone. When mixed with mohair (a goat fiber) or suri (an alpaca fiber), wool yarns have an airy vibe that creates a beautiful halo on the sweater. In some regions, such as Iceland, yarns gravitate toward more rustic wool to create airtight sweaters that can stand up to the harsh terrain of their climate and keep with tradition.

SHEEP'S WOOL VS. CAMELID (ALPACA AND LLAMA)

While still technically wool, I wanted to talk about alpaca and llama yarns because their properties can affect the garment you're working on. First, llama yarn is much coarser and typically is used in rugs. I'd avoid making a sweater with it. Alpaca, on the other hand, has a lot of benefits. While sheep's wool contains air pockets and can easily bounce back into shape due to its crimps and elasticity, alpaca fibers are completely hollow and longer, with fewer crimps per inch. This makes them super lightweight and perfect for designs that need to be on the lighter end of the scale, such as a long duster or tunic-length sweater (simply because of combating gravity). But note: This quality also makes alpaca prone to stretching, so you'll need to consider this when blocking. Since the length of each fiber is longer, it creates a beautiful drape that can be harder to achieve with other fibers. Other reasons why you might like alpaca: since it's lanolin-free (meaning it doesn't have the oils produced from the sheep on its wool), it's also hypoallergenic. This makes it a great sub for those who have sheep's wool allergies.

SUPERWASH WOOL

Superwash wool is a great alternative for those who want the warmth of wool but like being able to throw their sweater into the washing machine—no having to hand wash it each time. One thing to note about superwash wool is that it does lose some of its structural properties in the superwash process, where the scales have either been removed or coated, so they cannot stick together. This process can also make the wool less itchy and softer, making it the perfect choice for baby or kids' clothes, but beware. While it is helpful with machine washing and drying, the downside to superwash wool is that it tends to grow quite a bit when it hits water, which is why you'll want to chuck it in the dryer for it to bounce back into shape.

Acrylic

Acrylic yarn is a manmade synthetic fiber that is known for being strong, durable, and lightweight. It also maintains its shape well. Since it's essentially made from polyacrylonitrile (plastic), this makes it easy to wash, open to some pretty rough use, and a great hypoallergenic option for those who have wool allergies. On the cost scale, acrylic yarns tend to be on the lower end while still being warm and machine washable. This makes them great for baby items, children's clothes, and for those loved ones in your family who will just throw your hand-knit gift into the dryer no matter how many times you tell them not to. While acrylics get a bad rap because they are not as ecofriendly as the rest of the wool options, they definitely have their place in the making world.

Plant-Based Fibers

Hello, hot-weather knits! Plant-based fibers are chosen for many reasons, but they usually come down to weather. Bamboo, cotton, and linen are all fibers that are known for being breathable, lightweight, and moisture-wicking. This makes them the perfect yarn for the summer season. Since these fibers tend to be long and not crimped (unlike wool), they have less memory, meaning they don't hold their shape well. However, with the loss of structure, they gain leaps and bounds in drape. So, while they may not be the best for a heavily structured garment or a long duster cardigan (due to having to battle with gravity constantly), they work extremely well for free-flowing tops and cardigans that don't need to retain heat.

Between many breeds of sheep, angora rabbits, cashmere goats, alpaca, acrylic, and plant-based fibers (to name a few), there are tons of different yarns to choose from, and they all have different properties and different reasons as to why you or the designer might pick them. As you choose yarns for your sweaters, keep these fiber properties in mind. The designer won't steer you wrong, but that doesn't mean you can't make your own choices.

ADDITIONAL THINGS TO CONSIDER

Beyond yarn weight and fiber content, there are a few other things to consider when substituting yarns. Let's talk through a few of those now.

Price point—Sweaters use a lot of yarn, particularly for larger sizes. The cost adds up. Choose a yarn at a price point that works best for your budget. Some yarns, such as cashmere, will naturally be on the higher end of the scale, and you may want to wait to splurge on knitting a cashmere sweater until you have a few sweaters under your belt.

The touch test—Everyone's skin reacts differently to various animal fibers. A "touch test" can help you decide if a yarn is going to be "next-to-skin soft." To do this, place the yarn on your cheek, your neck, and along your collar to see if you like how it feels on these sensitive parts of your body. Get the heebie-jeebies? Sub it out for another yarn.

Environmental impact—Some knitters want to knit as ecofriendly as possible. Regarding the environmental impact of yarns, some of your options will be better than others. At a very high level, here are things to consider:

- Wool is a biodegradable, animal fiber.
- Acrylic is plastic and releases microplastics into our water system when washed.
- Plant-based fibers are biodegradable but use quite large amounts of water in their production.

Density—Some yarn is heavier than others because of how dense the yarn is by weight. For example, cotton tends to be quite a bit heavier than wool or alpaca. So even if you had the same amount of yards, the grams of the cotton would be heavier than the other two. Be aware that it might affect the drape and overall weight of your piece.

Texture—The texture of the yarn you go with can create a completely different look than the sample knit. Boucle, mohair, faux fur, thick-thin, roving, woolen spun, worsted spun . . . all can affect your stitch definition or can hide or make elements pop within the design.

Dye lots—While larger companies tend to dye the same color in larger batches because they have the capacity, smaller companies might only be able to dye in smaller batches. These batches are called "dye lots" and you will want to try your best to purchase the same dye lot for your whole sweater. If you run out of yarn while knitting your project, try to purchase the same dye lot as before so you don't have subtle color differences halfway through your knit.

Colors—When choosing what color to make your garment in, consider the stitch choices in the design. Solid colors may show off lace and texture stitches more than a variegated yarn, while darker colors might drown out the cables in your pattern. For colorwork designs, you want to pick colors that have high contrast from one another, so the design really pops.

YARNSUB.COM

After you've read all that information, I am now going to give you a shortcut, which is yarnsub.com. Yarnsub.com is a website where you can plunk in the yarn the designer used, and it will assimilate all of the info and factors from above to spit out some yarn substitute suggestions for you. While it doesn't consider your budget or what's local to you, and it doesn't have every yarn catalogued in its base, it is a great place to start.

SAY NO TO YARN SNOBS

Whether you're in a Facebook group or just simply sharing your work at your craft night or on social media, there will always be yarn snobs wanting to weigh in on your yarn choices. My advice? Ignore them. There are a lot of factors that play a role in yarn subbing and the main thing to know is that *you need to do what's best for you*. So go forth, my yarn-subbing master. You've got this . . . and if you don't, you can always rip out and try it again with another yarn!

TLDR-Too long. Didn't read.

Picking your yarn is half the fun of knitting up your project, but some factors may influence whether you want to use the exact yarn that's called for in the pattern or if you want to sub it out.

Yarn subbing: Depending on a range of reasons (such as availability in your region, wanting to use up your stash, allergies, or personal preferences), you can either choose to use the yarn suggested in a pattern or substitute it for another. If you choose to yarn sub, you will want to compare a few things:

Yarn weight—Yarn comes in multiple weight classes that can be distinguished by a number (size 4 or #4), a size name (worsted weight, bulky weight), or occasionally by ply (2-ply, 4-ply, 5-ply jumper weight). There are subcategories to each weight class, and you can use math to determine if they are close. While you can technically yarn sub with a different weight yarn, it is highly discouraged as it can throw off the fit of your piece and may require you to rewrite the pattern's math on your own.

Fiber content—Different fibers (such as wool, superwash wool, camelid, acrylic, and plant-based fibers) have different characteristics when knit up. While some are sturdy and bounce back with memory (wool), others have little to no memory and can stretch and react differently to gravity (plant-based). Some are machine washable and great for projects such as baby and kids' clothes (superwash), while others are hypoallergenic, making them the perfect choice for those with allergies (acrylic). Designers usually choose certain fibers for drape, feel, aesthetic, or season, so you can either try and stay as close to the fiber content as possible (which is what I suggest), or you can play around.

Other things you will want to consider while yarn subbing are price point, how it feels on your skin, how ecofriendly it is, fiber density, texture, color, and dye lots. Overall, when choosing a yarn substitute, there are many things that come into play, but the most important is that it has to work for you! Just make sure you make a gauge swatch to check that it will work and give you the fabric you desire. The worst-case scenario is that it doesn't work out. In that case, you can simply frog it (take it apart) and start anew.

SIX

Gauge Swatching

The dreaded gauge swatch . . . just kidding, I promise it isn't as scary as it sounds and is sometimes made out to be. That being said, a gauge swatch is very important when it comes to knitting a sweater and that's because we want our sweaters to fit! While somewhat trivial for scarves and items that are okay varying from the required finished measurements, so much of the sizing of garments relies on this 4 × 4-inch (10 × 10 cm) square. So, let's break it down easy-peasy. In this chapter, we are going to go through what a gauge swatch is, the purpose of it, how to make one, what to do if your gauge swatch doesn't match, and tips and tricks along the way.

WHAT IS A GAUGE SWATCH?

A gauge swatch is essentially a 4 × 4-inch (10 × 10 cm) swatch of fabric in the main stitch of the pattern of the project that shows the knitter's tension. While some knitters are naturally tighter, others are looser since we all wrap and tug our yarn a little differently on our needles. Since patterns are made by the designers themselves, swatching is a way of making sure we all get the same size stitches, both in width and height, before starting the pattern.

For example, say that we are both knitting with the same worsted-weight yarn and with the same U.S. size 15 (10 mm) needles. *Technically,* a single stitch should be 10 mm wide and 10 mm tall. But if I am a looser knitter, my stitches might be bigger simply because of how loosely I drape my yarn over the needle. However, you might be a tighter knitter and tug at the end of the stitch, cinching the hole of the stitch to be less than 10 mm in diameter. (This is one of those times where metric units make an explanation easier than imperial. Trust me, you don't want to measure .39 of an inch.) Essentially, we need to find a way to get to the same diameter, even if we knit looser or tighter.

WHY IS A SWATCH IMPORTANT?

Designers grade their patterns (a.k.a. do the math to find the stitch counts for other sizes outside of their samples) by using their gauge swatch as a foundation. Pattern sizes historically expand in the bust by a 4-inch (10-cm) difference in each size, which means that, rudimentarily, designers are adding a gauge swatch of fabric in width for each size. If a knitter doesn't match the designer's gauge and is off by a few stitches, this will start to compound, resulting in either a smaller or bigger fit.

Making a gauge swatch is not as annoying as other knitters make it out to be, and it will make your sweaters fit better, so do it.

HOW TO DO A GAUGE SWATCH

First, you'll need to find the designer's gauge in the pattern and see how many stitches and rows it calls for. This is normally at the start of the pattern—beware of a pattern that *doesn't* tell you the gauge! Cast on that number of stitches, plus a few extra for each side, onto your needles and knit the suggested number of rows, plus a few more. Bind off your gauge swatch, measure it with a measuring tape, and write down what you got for your pre-blocked gauge. Note: The gauge swatch in the pattern will always be a "blocked" gauge swatch. Measuring your swatch before and after blocking can show a significant change in gauge. At this time, you should block your gauge swatch using the same method you plan on using to block your finished piece and write down your post-blocked gauge. Flip to page 67 to learn all about blocking and then come on back!

WHAT TO DO IF YOUR GAUGE SWATCH IS NOT THE SAME

Don't panic! This is pretty common, and the easy solution is to switch your needle size and try again. While both are important, when it comes to gauge swatches, your stitch count is going to take precedence over your row count. This is simply because adding width in the middle of a pattern is much harder than adding or subtracting length. This gets a bit trickier when it comes to raglans and yokes, but it is better to be safe than sorry and err on the side of your stitch count being more accurate.

There are two main scenarios that may occur when your gauge swatch doesn't match. You'll either have too many stitches in that 4 × 4-inch (10 × 10 cm) square or too little. Here's what to do:

What to Do If You Have More Stitches in Width and Row Count

Let's say the gauge swatch calls for 12 stitches (sts) × 16 rows, but you get 14 sts × 18 rows. This means that your stitches are smaller and shorter because you can fit more in the span of 4 inches (10 cm). This also means you're a tighter knitter than the designer. In this case, you will want to bump *up* a needle size or two to make bigger stitches and try your gauge swatch again. If your next gauge swatch is 13 sts × 17 rows, keep bumping up a needle size until you get the correct gauge in the pattern. Don't forget to block your swatch because sometimes stitches grow and "bloom." So, you might be totally fine and ready to cast on.

What to Do If You Have Fewer Stitches in Width and Row Count

Let's use the same example where the gauge swatch calls for 12 sts × 16 rows, but you get 10 sts × 14 rows. This means that your stitches are too wide, and your rows are too tall because you can't fit as many in the span of 4 inches (10 cm). This also means you're a looser knitter than the designer. In this case, you will want to bump *down* a needle size or two to make smaller stitches and try your gauge swatch again. If your gauge doesn't land on

Measure left to right for stitch gauge and top to bottom for row gauge.

Sizing & Gauge Swatches

We've all been there. You do your gauge swatch and it's like . . . 1–2 stitches off. You think, "Eh, it's close enough." *Stop!* While those 1–2 stitches may sound minimal, they can wreak havoc on your final fit, especially as we gwet into the plus sizes. Because of the way sweater designs are graded (where a designer takes their sample size and their gauge swatch to determine the stitch count for all other sizes), an incorrect gauge will disproportionally affect plus sizes, mainly because that gauge error will begin to compound more quickly.

Let's Play a Gwame:

I want you to imagine that you get $10 given to you each day for a week, totaling $70. If you spend $12 in the first day, you'll end up taking away $2 from the next day. If you spend $12 the following day and then $12 again and again, always borrowing another $2 from the next day, you won't have any money left for the last day of the week. You'll have run out of money on day 5.8 out of 7. This happens in knitting too!

Now imagine that each day is a 10-stitch gauge swatch, and the dollars are stitches. Each day, you've spent an additional ¾ inches (2 cm) worth of fabric, totaling over 4 inches (10 cm) worth of fabric that has disappeared at the end of the round. You've essentially removed the difference of a whole garment size. Yikes!

Let's Put This into Reality in a Knitting Example:

Let's say the designer is a size medium (hi, that's me!) and they must do their 4-inch (10 cm) swatch 9 times around to get a 36-inch (91.5 cm) circumference. If you were also a medium and your gauge was 12 stitches instead of 10, you would end up with a 30-inch (76 cm) circumference instead. That's a 6-inch (15 cm) difference. That's pretty big!

This issue only compounds more and more on sizes as they go up or down. To demonstrate this even farther, we are going to do a wee bit of designing. If I am a medium and I cast on 90 sts for my size, that would mean that the large would cast on 100 stitches, the XL would cast on 110, the 2XL would cast on 120, and so on and so forth. But by not landing gauge and getting 12 stitches instead of 10, the large would end up being 6¾ inches (17 cm) smaller than intended, the XL would be 7¼ inches (18.5 cm) smaller than intended, and the 2XL would be 8 inches (20 cm) smaller than intended. It only progressively continues.

This is why it's always best to adjust our gauge swatches and do them again if they don't match, even if it takes us more time.

that next try, not to worry, you can always try again. Plus, you can totally reuse the yarn from your gauge swatches, so don't be afraid to continue to gauge swatch. Again, don't forget to block your swatch because sometimes stitches grow and "bloom." So, you might be totally fine and ready to cast on.

TIPS AND TRICKS FOR GAUGE SWATCHING

1. Cast on more stitches than the gauge states and work more rows. This way, you have a good selection of stitches to measure accurately without the edges warping or being muddled.

2. Cast on in the direction the pattern tells you. If it says to knit in the round, knit your swatch in the round. If it tells you to knit flat, knit flat. These small changes can make a big difference in your stitch size.

3. Block your swatch in the way you'll be blocking your finished piece. Different yarn fibers will react differently to different blocking methods, so you want to make sure you're blocking your gauge swatch to get an idea of how the yarn will react. Note your gauge before, and then after. Write that down.

4. Don't streeeeetch or squish your stitches while measuring. Your swatch should simply be lying on a flat surface. Not your knee. Even though I know you want to.

5. Check your gauge as you knit up your garment. Sometimes life happens and we shift into a tighter or looser tension as we knit. Keep tabs on your gauge throughout the pattern. Note that if your pre-blocked gauge is different than your post-blocked gauge, you might have to adjust the number of rows you work, knowing your piece may grow when blocked at the end.

TLDR-Too long. Didn't read.

The moral of the story is that gauge swatching is essential. It's okay to be a few stitches off for a scarf, but when it comes to a garment, getting the correct gauge means getting the proper measurements and fit for your sweater or cardigan. Gauge swatching is essentially a tension swatch, where we try to match the designer's tension. Some of us are tighter knitters; some of us are looser knitters. If we don't match the designer's gauge, we can simply adjust our needle size to get the correct stitch and row count.

P.S. Don't forget to block, then measure your gauge.

is done to make your piece divisible by four and evenly split your front, back, and arm sections. You will now have 196 (212, 228, 240, 256) (272, 288, 300, 316) sts.
60 (67, 72, 77, 82) (87, 92, 97, 102) sts
Front
Sleeve B
Sleeve A
38 (39, 42, 43, 46) (49, 52, 53, 56) sts
Back
BOR
Diagram illustrating your stitch counts before CO under arms. Viewed from the top of your piece.
Separate Body and Sleeves
Next, the body and sleeves need to be separated. Your sleeve stitches (Sleeve A and Sleeve B) will be placed on hold with waste yarn (using a darning needle, thread waste yarn through the live sts). The remainder of the body is knit in the round next. Note where your BOR is. You will start here!
Place first 38 (39, 42, 43, 46) (49, 52, 53, 56) sts on waste yarn for right sleeve, using backward loop method CO 3 (4, 4, 5, 6) (7, 7, 11, 11) sts, place new BOR marker, CO 3 (3, 4, 4, 6) (6, 7, 10, 11) sts, K60 (67, 72, 77, 82) (87, 92, 97, 102) sts for front, place 38 (39, 42, 43, 46) (49, 52, 53, 56) sts on waste yarn for left sleeve, using backward loop method CO 6 (7, 8, 9, 12) (13, 14, 21, 22) sts, K all sts until end of round for back. With the sleeves now on hold, you will have 132 (148, 160, 172, 188) (200, 212, 236, 248) sts for the body.
BODY
K all sts until the body measures 4" (10 cm) from the underarm.
Waist Shaping
Set-up Rnd: K66 (74, 80, 86, 94) (100, 106, 118, 124), PM, K until end of round.
Decrease Rnd: K4, K2tog, K until 6 sts before marker, SSK, K4, SM, K4, K2tog, K until last 6 sts, SSK, K4. (4 sts decreased.)
You now have 128 (144, 156, 168, 184) (196, 208, 232, 244) sts.
K all sts until the body measures 3" (7.5) cm past the decrease round. Repeat the decrease round. You now have 124 (140, 152, 164, 180) (192, 204, 228, 240) sts.
K all sts until the body measures 1" (2.5 cm) past the last decrease round.
Increase Rnd: K4, M1L, K until 4 sts before marker, M1R, M4, SM, K4, M1L, K until last 4 sts, M1R, K4. (4 sts increased.)

SEVEN

How to Read a Pattern

Phew, you're almost ready to cast on! You've learned a schwackload of stuff up to here, and now it's time to pick up your pattern and get started. But . . . you look at it, and your jaw drops . . . how the heck are you supposed to even *read* this? It's like a completely different language. You start to panic and think maybe you have bitten off more than you can chew. *Stop!* Take a deep breath; you've got this.

When I first looked at a pattern, I thought I was staring at a page full of Klingon. So many numbers, so many letters, so many things. It got overwhelming. But the best thing to know before deep diving into this chapter is that patterns are worked in chunks. We break them down as we go, and you will do the same.

START WITH A READ THROUGH

First things first, read through the pattern from start to finish. Many designers develop a set pattern style unique to them, so you won't always find the same information in the same place in the pattern. Some may have all the essential information on the first page, others might sprinkle it throughout. While you shouldn't go too deep into exactly how every single row works, you should get a good sense of how the pattern is constructed and flows. Designers usually try their best to answer any of the questions that might pop up for you within different portions of the pattern. So, it's helpful to read the pattern from start to finish before casting on.

Let's go through common elements seen in almost every pattern:

Photos—Patterns include a variety of photos showing the project so you can see how the garment looks from various angles and to illustrate details close up.

List of tools and materials—Most patterns provide a basic list of the tools (needles and which size, notions like stitch markers and scissors) and materials (yarn, buttons, and so on) you need so you can have everything on hand before you start.

Gauge—You should always see the gauge listed in the pattern. This is to ensure you know the designer's tension so you can match it and get the same final measurements of your garment. Read Chapter 6 (p. 47) if you need a refresher.

Schematics or finished measurements—These provide a visual reference and exact dimensions of the finished garment. The schematic helps you visualize the end

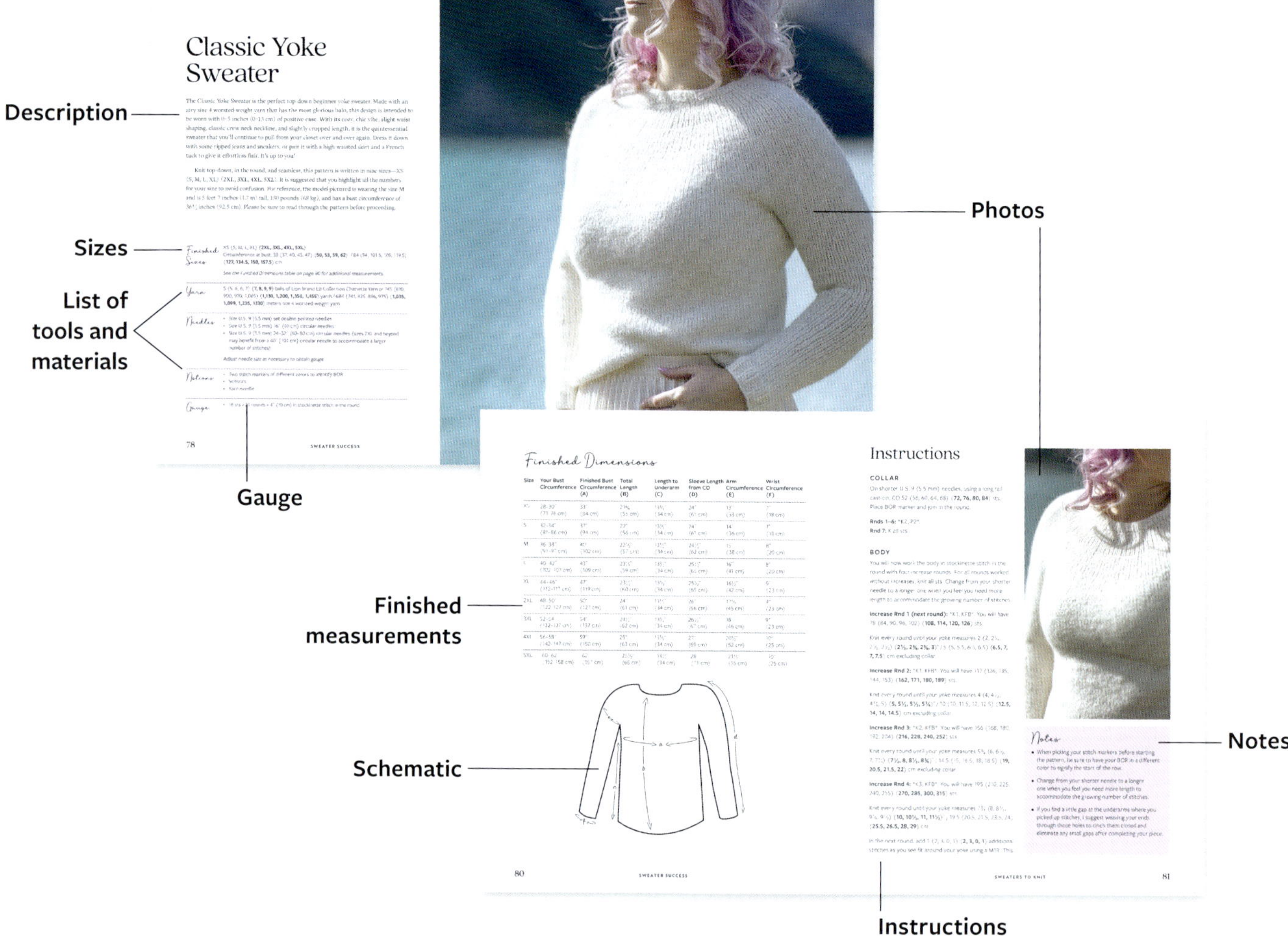

product by showing how the measurements will correspond to different parts of the piece.

Stitch guide/glossary/abbreviations—Since patterns are written in shorthand, having a glossary of abbreviations will let you know what each acronym stands for, while a stitch guide may explain how to do certain stitches. (You'll find all the abbreviations for this book on p. 130.)

Description and notes—This is a place where designers will add additional information that they may not be able to place within the pattern, much like a catch-all. It's helpful to always read the description and notes sections.

Instructional text—The instructions are a.k.a. the actual pattern directions. Just like it says, you will find the written-out steps (much like a recipe) to making the project so you can work your piece from start to finish.

While all patterns aren't created equal, these are the basics. If one of these things is missing, beware. You might need to take some educated guesses for anything lacking or forgotten in that pattern.

MAKE SURE YOU UNDERSTAND THE ABBREVIATIONS

In knitting and crochet patterns, you'll find a lot of abbreviations. This is usually where the overwhelm begins because the pattern in shortform tends to look like a totally different language than we speak. But it's really done for the purpose of shortening the length of the pattern. For example, instead of writing out the word "knit" a million times, designers will shorten this to "K." Go through the glossary and start to familiarize yourself with each abbreviation. See one you don't recognize? That's okay! Head to Google or YouTube and give it a quick search. That way, you have an idea of how those stitches are worked in advance before you even get to them. Also know that you can return to the glossary for reference at any point, and you can bring up those tutorials on YouTube whenever you need them.

FOCUS ON YOUR SIZE

Unlike patterns with only one size and stitch count to follow, such as a scarf, garment patterns have all the sizes written at once. Many makers will start to balk at seeing all these numbers, not knowing which ones to follow. While there are some variations for each designer, you can expect something like this in the reference section on finished sizes: XS (S, M, L, XL) (**2X, 3X, 4X, 5X**). This corresponds to lines in the pattern that read like this: K5 (5, 7, 7, 8) (**10, 10, 12, 15**). You'll want to follow the numbers that correspond to your size and *only* those numbers. This means you can essentially ignore the rest as you knit. In this case, if you are knitting a size 4X, you knit 12 stitches.

BREAK YOUR PATTERN INTO SECTIONS

Chances are, your pattern will already have headers with different sections, such as the yoke instructions for raglans and circular yokes, arms/sleeves, torsos, hems, and so on. This is a great way to focus on one thing without being too overwhelmed by the rest. The overall sentiment of knitting a whole sweater can be daunting, but when we break it down into *just* the sleeves, or *just* the collar, or *just* the back panel, it shifts our mindset into a more positive and confident one. Don't be afraid to do this within sections, too!

TRACK YOUR WORK AND ADD NOTES

Whether you are reading your pattern, making notes and scribbles, check-marking, using a row counter on a printed document, or following along and marking off sections as you go in an app like knitCompanion, it's always best to track where you are in the pattern and make note of anything you may have changed. Should you decide to put the project down for a short or long period, you'll always know where you are when you come back to it. Your future self will thank you!

Highlighters Can Help!

If you have a printed copy of your pattern, highlight or circle your size's stitch counts throughout the whole pattern. That way your eyes will be trained to only follow those numbers and to not get distracted by the others. While you're at it, physically cross out the sections that may not pertain to you. For example, you may find some of the patterns in this book have certain sizes that branch off into a different set of instructions. So, if you come to a section that reads **"Sizes XS-L Only,"** but you are working up size XL, you can cross that section out in advance so you don't accidentally work it when coming to that section of the pattern.

*Note: If you are getting this book from the library, please please please don't be a d*ck and do NOT write in the book itself. My husband, who's a library technician, would shudder.*

TECHNICAL TIPS

Now, let's get to the technical parts! Throughout each pattern, you will see various symbols and graphics pop up in multiple places. Whether it's for telling you a certain stitch sequence, indicating what stitches to repeat and for how many times, or giving additional information, these symbols help break up each row into bite-size pieces. Rather than writing them out in long form and, in doing so, possibly convoluting the pattern, these symbols help shorten the overall pattern while making it easier to read . . . once you understand them. Note that some of these overlap one another and some designers use some interchangeably. Get to know the writer's style, and you should become more familiar with time.

Commas

Throughout your pattern, you'll see rows where a set of commas break down each step. I like to think of these commas as stop signs. You'll look to see what the next step is, work those stitches, then *stop*. Then you'll take a peek at what the pattern tells you to do next, take a breath, and assess if you know how to do that technique. If you don't? Head over to YouTube or give it a quick Google search to get acquainted. Then, you'll work that set of instructions until the next comma and repeat. This helps break down each row in a way that is more manageable and less stress-inducing.

Asterisks

Asterisks are broken down into single asterisks or double asterisks. Single asterisks show where the beginning of the repeat starts, while double asterisks show the beginning and end of that repeat.

Example of a single asterisk:
Row 1: *K1, P1, repeat from * until the end of row.

This example tells us to knit one stitch then purl one stitch in a repeating pattern until we reach the end of the row. The start of the repeat is K1 and it ends with P1. You will repeat knit one purl one over and over again until the end of the row. This repeat creates a 1 × 1 rib.

Example of a double asterisk:
Row 1: *K2, P2* across.

This example tells us that we will knit two then purl two and repeat those four stitches. The two asterisks flank the repeat, signaling what to do. We start the repeat with a K2 and end it with a P2. Even though it doesn't say "repeat from * to * until the end of the row," it is implied that it's worked with this repeat until you have worked all the stitches in that row. This repeat creates a 2 × 2 rib.

Brackets

Much like the asterisks, brackets break down a certain section of the pattern and let us know how many times that section needs to be repeated. Note that with brackets, they will always have a qualifier after them that tells you how many times a series of stitches needs to be repeated.

Example:
Row 1: K2, [K1, P1, K1] 3 times, K2.

This tells us that the total amount of stitches will be worked over 13 stitches, with the repeats happening in the middle 9 stitches. It translates to: knit two stitches, knit one stitch, purl one stitch, knit one stitch, knit one stitch, purl one stitch, knit one stitch, knit one stitch, purl one stitch, knit one stitch, then knit two stitches. (You see why we use abbreviations.) Here, it's much easier to say that you'll start the row with K2, work the stitches within the brackets three times, then end with K2.

Remember when we talked about stitch markers (p. 35)? This is a great place to use them. Place a marker after the first two stitches knit, then one after each repeat, and then you should have two stitches at the end. Each time you come to a marker, you know to restart the series of K1, P1, K1.

Parentheses

Parentheses are most often used to indicate a sequence of moves that will occur in the next stitch (such as making bobbles or popcorn stitches). What happens within the parentheses happens in just *one* stitch. Occasionally, they are used by the designer to give more information, too.

Example:
Row 1: K2, (K1, P1, K1), K2, (K1, P1, K1), K2.

This row is worked over 8 stitches and will increase to 12 stitches by the end. The (K1, P1, K1) series is three moves worked into one stitch to create a bobble or textured stitch. In your mind, it might make more sense to picture: K2, [make bobble], K2, [make bobble], K2. Another way the designer might present this is as a kfbf, which would appear as a special stitch in the glossary. Kfbf means to knit in the front, back, and front of a single stitch. Using that term, the row would read: K2, kfbf, K2, kfbf, K2.

But parentheses can also indicate more information that the designer wants to convey.

Example:
Row 1: K2, K2tog (2 times), K2.

This row is worked over 8 stitches and decreases to 6 stitches by the end of the row. Here, the parentheses tell you to repeat the K2tog over the middle four stitches twice.

Is this starting to make sense? Asterisks, brackets, and parenthesis can seem a bit scary when you first see them, but the more they pop up in your patterns, the more reading them will become second nature.

WHAT TO DO IF YOU GET STUCK

We all get stuck in patterns, and with garments having that many more details within them, it's bound to happen at some point. Sometimes, we either don't understand the directions, we don't know the technique and it's new for us, or we've given the row a go, but we don't have the right stitch count at the end. You're not alone!

Here are some things to do when troubleshooting.

1. Take a deep breath and trust the pattern! Most designers have either gotten their patterns tested by volunteers or tech edited by a magical yarn fairy editor (mine for this book is Sandi!), and sometimes they get both. When we overcomplicate things or jump ahead thinking we know what's best, taking a breath and walking away for a bit can make a massive difference.
2. Check multiple sections of the pattern (like the description and notes) to see if the designer addresses the problem you've encountered.
3. Scan the pattern for pictures or links that may have been provided.

4. Check Google and YouTube to see if you're doing a technique correctly.

5. Unknit (a.k.a. *tink*) that row back and try it again. You'd be surprised how often it works on the second try.

6. Check out sources such as Ravelry for other people's experiences and projects, and research to see if there have been any errata shared (meaning that there was an error in the pattern and it has been updated elsewhere).

7. Reach out to the designer with the pattern name, the section, the page number, and the paragraph/row you are having issues with. (Giving them all this information upfront will help eliminate back-and-forth messages, getting you an answer in a timely manner.) Disclaimer: Not all designers are responsive.

8. Last but not least, nothing beats in-person help, so head to your local yarn shop and see if someone there can help you. Local yarn shop staff are a wealth of knowledge and are a great resource in the community that can give hands-on help. Go with humility and an open heart just in case you've made a mistake. It happens to the best of us.

TLDR- Too long. Didn't read.

Reading a pattern can be daunting. With abbreviations, multiple stitch counts, and so many details to follow, it's no wonder that a pattern can look like a totally different language . . . because it technically is. It's the language of knitting! That being said, it's nothing to be afraid of. Everything can be broken down into bite-sized chunks, and patterns are no different.

When going through a pattern, you can expect to see some basic things, such as: photos, a list of tools and materials, gauge, schematics and measurements, glossaries and abbreviations, and descriptions or notes, along with the actual written pattern itself. It's a lot of information to take in, but here are some tips for reading your first pattern:

- Read through from start to finish.
- Familiarize yourself with the abbreviations in the glossary.
- Focus on your size only by highlighting or circling the stitch count of your size throughout the pattern.
- Treat every comma like a stop sign. See the comma, stop, reassess the next steps, work those stitches, and repeat.
- Get familiar with how asterisks, brackets, and parentheses work in a pattern.
- Track where you are within your pattern and add notes as you go.
- If you get stuck, that's okay. It happens to the best of us, and there are many ways to troubleshoot, such as taking a breath and stepping away, trusting the pattern and forging ahead, tinking back and trying the row again, scanning the pattern and notes for any tips the designer might have given for this section, reaching out to the designer, or heading into your local yarn shop to get some hands-on help.

Reading a pattern can seem scary initially, but the more you break it down into manageable chunks, the better you will feel. Just know that this is something new for you, and new can be scary. Give yourself some props. You must start somewhere. There's only up from here!

EIGHT

Making Mods

You've mastered how to read a pattern, but did you know you can also *change* it to better fit or suit your style? As a designer, I am a firm believer that patterns should be used as blueprints because that's the best part about making your own clothes—you can tailor them to your body and aesthetic! You can add length or take it away, move stitch counts, and make other adjustments to get the right fit or the vibe you want. Unlike sewing, knitters and crocheters have an advantage since we can simply frog something and try it again if it doesn't work. In this chapter, we will mainly be going into how to modify a pattern to fit your body better, but you can also use these tools to alter a pattern to your own personal flair. I'll preface this chapter with this: Many new knitters feel nervous about manipulating patterns, but once you do it the first time, it's highly addictive, and the world is your oyster.

Before you start altering a pattern, it's good to understand how the original project was designed and made. As we talked about in chapter 3 (p. 27), designers base their sizes off bust/chest measurements, and these measurements are based on standardized sizing, such as Craft Yarn Council (CYC) standards. It's important to remind ourselves again as we reach for that tape measure that standards are *just standards*, and not everyone (including myself!) fits the "standard" across the board. Table 1 on page 24 is a starting point. When taking your measurements and comparing to the chart, you're likely to see where you want to make alterations.

I suggest comparing your personal measurements to the following in the table on page 24:

- Bust
- Waist
- Hips
- Upper arm circumference
- Arm length
- Torso length

As you're going through these, note the places where your measurements vary from CYC. For example, I have a bust of 36.5 inches (92 cm), which places me firmly in the M category for a sweater, since garment sizes are mainly based on bust/chest circumference. This will be the size I choose to knit. However, my waist is 31 inches (79 cm), putting my measurements between an M and L, and my hips are 42 inches (107 cm), which 100% lands in the L territory. What does this mean? It means I have a better idea of where to adjust and play with a pattern to make it fit better.

BODY SHAPE

As you're taking your measurements, you'll probably start to notice something: When compared side by side, the measurements will start to make shapes. No, we will not compare you to an apple or a pear (hello, that is dumb, antiquated, and you are not a piece of fruit!), but seeing your body measurements in relationship to each other can help you figure out where you might want to make modifications.

Rectangle

Anatomy: From the top down, your bust, waist, and hips are all similar in measurements and proportions.

Possible mods: You may want to eliminate any waist shaping altogether on tight knits or add them to oversized knits to create the illusion of shaping.

Inverted Triangle

Anatomy: From the top down, your bust is larger than your waist, and your waist is larger than your hips.

Possible mods: Depending on the construction of your knit, you might want to cast on for one size and then transition to another.

Triangle

Anatomy: From the top down, your bust is smaller than your waist, and your waist is smaller than your hips.

Possible mods: Much like the inverted triangle, you might want to cast on for a different size and transition to another. An example is casting on a bigger size to accommodate your hips in a bottom-up sweater and gradually changing to a smaller size for your bust.

Hourglass

Anatomy: From the top down, your bust and hips are larger than your waist.

Possible mods: You may want to add waist shaping in oversized knits or play with ease to get the look you want.

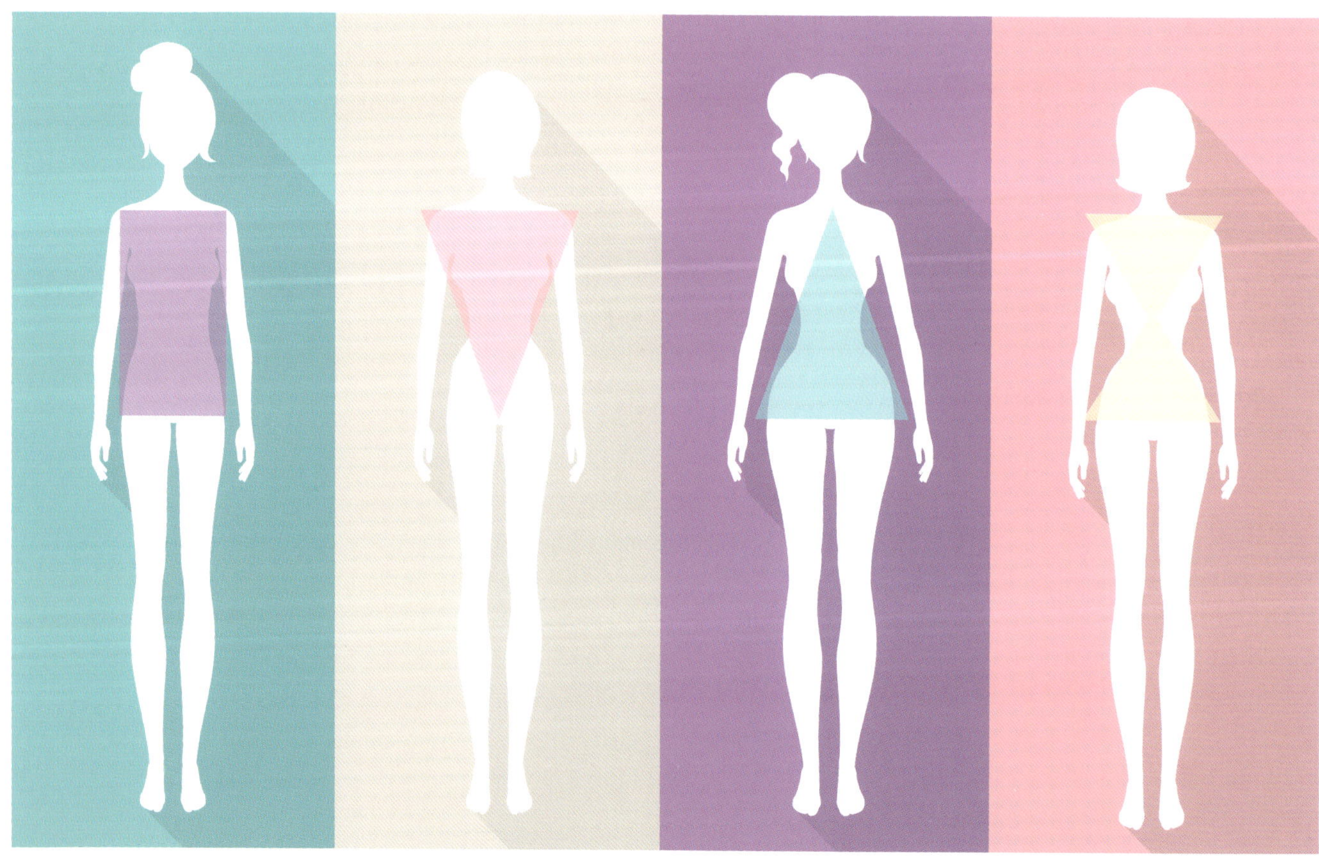

While I have outlined potential modifications for each body shape, any of these mods can be done on any body shape, but this is a good place to start thinking out of the box of what the possibilities are.

HOW TO MODIFY

With an idea in mind of *what* you want to modify (like adding length in the torso or sleeves, adding waist shaping, or transitioning sizes within the same pattern), let's chat about *how* to modify it. I know you'll hate me, but it all comes down to your gauge swatch and math.

Simply put, patterns work based on a set number of stitches and number of rows. I like to think of this along the lines of sewing a garment. If you add more stitches or more rows, you add more fabric. If you take out stitches or take out rows, you have less fabric. When a designer is grading a pattern (fancy talk for writing it in multiple sizes), they are essentially adding and subtracting the amount of "fabric" that needs to fit over each size's measurements. By industry standard, sizes go in increments of 4 inches (10 cm), and guess what else is 4 inches (10 cm)? **Your gauge swatch.** With a bit of math, you can start to change, alter, and manipulate any pattern to work in your favor.

Want to add an inch in length? Use your gauge swatch to figure out how many rows to add. Need to take out an inch in width here? Use your gauge swatch to figure out how many stitches you need to decrease.

Example Adding or Removing Length

Your gauge swatch is 16 stitches × 20 rows for a 4 × 4-inch (10 × 10 cm) square. To figure out how many rows are needed to add 1 inch (2.5 cm) of length, divide 20 rows by 4 inches (10 cm). This tells you that your row gauge is 5 rows per 1 inch (2.5 cm). So, you'll want to knit 5 more rows. If you want to remove 1 inch (2.5 cm) of length, you will know to stop 5 rows early.

Example Adding Width

Based on the same 16 stitches × 20 rows for a 4 × 4-inch (10 × 10 cm) square gauge, let's look at how to add 1 inch (2.5 cm) to the width. To figure out how many stitches to add, divide 16 stitches by 4 inches (10 cm). This tells you that your stitch gauge is 4 stitches per 1 inch (2.5 cm). So, you will want to add 4 stitches to your stitch count. This works in reverse as well. If you want to remove 1 inch (2.5 cm) of fabric, decrease by 4 stitches.

COMMON MODIFICATIONS

Adding a Size That Isn't Written

Have you seen a pattern you love but it isn't written for your size? You can use the pattern gauge and your gauge swatch to calculate the stitches you need for your size. Let's work through an example.

Your gauge and the pattern's gauge are the same: 16 stitches × 20 rows for a 4 × 4-inch (10 × 10 cm) square. The pattern tops out at size L, and you need an XL. The pattern says to cast on 100 stitches for the L. Mathematically, the XL would cast on an additional 16 stitches, making it 116. The next size would cast on 132, then 148, and so on and so forth, always adding another "gauge swatch" worth of fabric.

It can get a bit tricky after that, as you will then need to redistribute the stitches as you work through the remainder of the pattern. Again, your gauge swatch will be helpful. If your sweater is a raglan, you may need to add another repeat (or two) to get to the stitches needed at your bust. Read ahead in the pattern. How many rows are worked between the cast on and separation for the sleeves for size L? What is that stitch count for the body after the sleeve separation? Is that your bust measurement, plus the recommended ease? Do the math. You got this!

It's important to note that some patterns have repeats that are worked over a certain number of stitches (like lacework, colorwork, or textural stitches), which means that your math may not work out perfectly. In this case, you may have to fudge it as best as you can! Just try to get to the number closest to that original gauge swatch increment while keeping these points in mind.

Adding or Eliminating Length

Since we are not all the same height with identical torsos and arm lengths, adjusting length is a great way to modify a pattern to make it work for your body, or alter it for your style preference. Adding or subtracting rows (based on your gauge swatch) in a pattern is an easy way to get a custom fit. As you knit, try it on as you go to temperature check and see if you're at your preferred length. Don't forget to consider your pre- and post-blocked gauge just in case they differ, and know that adding length will require more yarn. Only you can decide where you want those hems or cuffs to end.

Waist Shaping

Waist shaping changes the shape of the body of your sweater below the underarm and above the bottom hem. Essentially, through increasing and decreasing the number of stitches in the torso section, you make the fabric go from wide to narrow and then back out again to follow the curvature of your body. To do this, you'll want to measure your torso length and note where your natural waist is in relation to the hem. Again, let's work through an example.

On average, waist shaping is worked over 7 inches (18 cm), 3 inches (8 cm) both above and below the waist, and 1 inch (2.5 cm) for the natural waistline. However, you'll want to check your own measurements to confirm this on your body. If you have a longer torso, use your gauge as a guide to add rows to each section, and vice versa for shortening. If you want to bring the waist in more than 1 inch (2.5 cm), your gauge swatch can tell you how many more decreases to add.

Underarm Shaping

Depending on the design construction (I'm looking at you, drop shoulders!), you might find that there is a lot of excess fabric bunching at the sides of your underarms, which can be uncomfortable, shatter any illusion of clean lines, and draw unwanted attention. This is especially prevalent in larger sizes, where designers can be overindulgent in the amount of fabric in the underarm area due to the stitch count that is needed to cover the bust measurement. Not to worry though: You can work underarm shaping. This is where you will eliminate additional fabric by decreasing stitches in the section between the underarm and the shoulder. By using your gauge swatch, determine how much fabric (a.k.a. how many stitches) you want to eliminate over how many rows. Then, start decreasing gradually on the sides that are closest to your arms.

The Classic Yoke Sweater (p. 78) has waist shaping built into the pattern.

Short-row shaping is used in the Simple Stockinette Raglan pattern (p. 86) to raise the back neckline.

In this book, the Neapolitan Pullover (p. 94), Ivy League Vest (p. 102), and Afternoon Tea Cardi (p. 110) patterns use this shaping form.

Short-Row Shaping

Short rows can be used in multiple places of your garment, such as shaping or raising necklines in top-down sweaters, adding bust darts (as seen in the next section), and shaping shoulders when working a sleeve. They are essentially partial rows where you work to a certain point in the row/round, then turn and work back across the stitches you just worked, and repeat, thus creating a wedge of additional fabric. Let's dive into the most common type of short-row shaping: raising the back neckline.

If you ever felt like you needed to pull your collar down because it was riding up, or the protrusion of your bust literally lifted the front hem of your sweater to reveal your stomach, this is where short rows can really work their magic. Short rows add length in the back, which results in tilting the collar down to land closer to your collar bones. The best place to add short rows is within 1 to 2 inches (2.5–5 cm) of the collar and above the underarm split. This may sound strange, but adding length to the back will allow the front to move down, which can rise when having to drape over the bust, resulting in the hem landing evenly. While it seems counter intuitive that adding length to only the back would add length to the front, it does work!

TLDR- Too long. Didn't read.

While garment patterns are based on standardized sizing (such as those set by the Craft Yarn Council) that doesn't mean that you can't use them like a blueprint. You can modify sizes to make a custom fit for your body.

Comparing your measurements to standards is a great way to see the areas you might want to modify. From rectangle to inverted triangle to regular triangle to hourglass, seeing how the measurements relate to each other can help you envision your body shape and see what modifications might be up your alley.

Some common modifications include lengthening or shortening torsos and arms, waist shaping, shoulder shaping, short rows, and bust darts. You can even add sizes to a pattern that weren't previously there. All these modifications are done by using math and your trusty gauge swatch. By the process of eliminating or adding rows or stitches, the world really is your oyster in creating the perfect fit and a style that is unique to you.

Bust Darts

Are you larger than an A or B cup? Chances are that bust darts might be helpful. They are especially great for those with larger busts that need more space and coverage in patterns. Bust darts create a curve and physically contour the fabric out to give the bust more room to breathe, and they work much like a heel turn in a sock.

There are two types of bust darts:

Horizontal—These are also known as "short-row bust darts." Worked exactly like the short rows above, they create an additional wedge to add length and coverage while contouring the shape of the fabric. Note: These should be worked at the apex of the bust to make sure the hem lies evenly.

Vertical—These are done by increasing and decreasing the number of stitches underneath and above your bust, so the fabric expands to accommodate the bust size. (Imagine the shape of an oval or marquise.) While they are a bit trickier since you must pay attention to your stitch count, I personally find them more invisible than a horizontal bust dart, and they cover the bust better.

NINE

Blocking Your Knits

Welcome to the blocking section! Whether you're popping in from the gauge chapter or you're ready to block your finished knit (eeek, how exciting), blocking is an important step on your path to sweater success that you don't want to skip.

WHAT IS BLOCKING?

Blocking is the process of bringing your finished project into contact with some form of water to set its shape, even out stitches, and "lock" in your measurements. However, it actually comes into play in two parts of your sweater journey: First, when you block your gauge swatch, and again when you block your finished piece.

BLOCKING YOUR SWATCH

Blocking your swatch is a great way to see how your yarn reacts in its final state. Does your yarn bloom? Does it grow? Do you like the fabric? Do you like the drape? Most yarns and gauge swatches tend to grow in size with blocking, so you'll want to make sure you're blocking your gauge swatch *and* your finished garment in the same fashion.

It's important to write down your pre- and post-blocked gauges, as you may need to adjust an element of your pattern while you're knitting your piece. For example, if you knit your swatch and it grows significantly, you will need to watch for patterns that say things like "knit to 8 inches (20 cm)." Why? Because a pattern based on lengths rather than row counts can be problematic when your yarn grows. If you knit for that length, your project might end up being 12 inches (30 cm) after it's blocked. I would hate for your unblocked piece to fit perfectly, to only block it and afterward it is too big. In this case, instead of knitting for 8 inches (20 cm), measure your row gauge after blocking. How many rows do you have to 1 inch (2.5 cm)? Multiply that by 8 (for the inches) and knit that many rows.

BLOCKING YOUR GARMENT AND WHY WE DO IT

Blocking your finished sweater does multiple things, but I really like to think that it's like hairspray for your knits. It's the final step that you take to keep your project in the right shape and dimensions. Just like you would hairspray your hair after curling it, the same goes for a sweater. You'll want to block it and lock it in place.

Tip You can't really block anything *smaller,* so be aware of this before you plunge your project in water!

Blocking also does the following things:

Evens out tension—As you knit, your tension will change ever so slightly. Whether you were stressed out one day or you just were feeling a little loosey-goosey another, when you pick up your piece you may notice that certain sections or one or two stitches aren't as uniform as another. Blocking helps smooth them out and gets them to lie flat and more evenly.

Blocking "relaxes" your wool—When you get your yarn, it can come in a range of forms—hanks, skeins, balls, cakes, and so on. Each of these yarn formats wraps and twists in different ways that will curl or kink your fiber due to how long they were in that shape. By blocking (wet blocking especially), the wool can "un-kink" and relax as it dries, leaving a more polished and orderly look.

Lets your stitches shine and reach their "max" potential—A lot of beautiful laceworks don't reveal their beauty until they've been blocked. By wetting the fabric and pulling the stitches open, the lace goes from eh to awesome. This also applies to cables and colorwork.

You're going to have to wash it anyway—You'll have to clean your piece at some point, so you'll want to block it anyway to ensure it stays in the size you want instead of stretching with use. Better to block and lock that size instead of letting it grow with gravity as you wear it and then have to block it at that larger size later.

BLOCKING TOOLS AND MATERIALS

We reviewed the supplies you'll need to block in a previous chapter (p. 36), but let's go over them again. There are lots of fun blocking tools out there. Here I've listed the most basic. Anything beyond these are nice to have, but aren't absolutely necessary.

Blocking pins—These help hold your project in place as it dries. Be sure to choose pins that will not rust, as the metal will be next to moisture when you block. I like Knitter's Pride Knit Blockers.

Blocking mats—These provide a flat surface to pin your garment on to.

There are many reasons why we block. Making your stitchwork shine is the biggest reason! Check out this swatch before (left) and after (right) blocking.

Absorbent towels—Regular cotton bath towels come handy when blocking. You'll use them to soak up some of the water before pinning the project out to dry.

Steamers, spray bottles, and water basins—Depending on how you plan to block your piece, you will need one or more of these items to be able to block your garment with water.

Nonrinse wool wash—Nonrinse wool wash will clean the oils and residue off your final piece without the additional agitation that happens when rinsing out traditional soap.

Water—All three methods use water, but if you can, try to use distilled water to eliminate mineral deposits.

THREE BLOCKING METHODS

There are three common ways to block your knits, all involving water in some shape or form: wet blocking, steam blocking, and mist blocking. Each method has pros and cons, but all lead to a more polished finished project. One important thing to keep in mind is that you can't really make your knits smaller through blocking, regardless of the approach you choose. So be aware before you start soaking!

How to Wet Block

Wet blocking is the method where you will fully submerge your knit in water. This is the best way to block your knits, as you plan on washing your garment later down the road. This process is also a great way to remove any oil residue from your hands left on the yarn while knitting it. You'll want tepid water and to limit the amount you touch your piece. Hot water and rubbing will agitate the fibers and they will felt together. You do not want this!

Here is the process to follow:

1. Fill a basin with tepid water and add about 1 teaspoon of nonrinse wool wash to the water. (I love the Eucalan one with the grapefruit smell.)
2. Swish to mix and get a good amount of suds.
3. Immerse your knit completely under the water and let sit for 20 minutes.

4. Carefully take the piece out and gently press out the water, making sure not to agitate the fiber by twisting and wringing it, or it will felt. Try not to let the weight of the water stretch your piece, either; imagine holding it like a fragile baby bird.

5. Lay your sweater flat on a towel, roll it up, and step on it to press out more water.

6. Place the garment on your blocking mats and pin it in place to the right dimensions.

7. Let 'er dry! To speed up the drying process, you can use a small fan to circulate the air.

How to Steam Block

Don't want to wait the lengthy time it takes for a wet block to dry? Steam blocking is a great option, though it doesn't work *as* well as a wet block.

1. Lay your knit out on your blocking mats and pin it into the final dimensions.

2. Turn your steamer (or the steam setting on your iron) onto the wool setting (or whichever setting works for the fiber you chose).

3. Holding the steamer roughly 1½–3 inches (4–8 cm) above your project, steam the item.

4. Run your hands over the steamed stitches to smooth them out.

5. Let dry.

You can also place a wet cloth on your item and press your iron/steamer into it. Note that heat will melt acrylic or fibers that are an acrylic blend, so be careful.

How to Mist Block

Like the steam block, mist blocking isn't as intensive as wet blocking, but it still gets the job done.

1. Lay your knit out on your blocking mats and pin into the final dimensions.

2. Mist your piece with a spray bottle until it's slightly but not overly damp.

3. Run your hands over the damp stitches to smooth them out.

4. Let dry.

TLDR- Too long. Didn't read.

Blocking comes into play in two parts of your sweater journey. First, you need to block your gauge swatch to check how your yarn reacts, and then you block your finished garment to lock it into the right dimensions.

Blocking also evens out the tension, relaxing your wool after it's been wound in a skein or hank. This gives your stitches the most potential to shine, in addition to working like "hairspray" for your knits by blocking and locking in the final dimensions you are looking for.

The process is easy. Though it's a step that most knitters don't like doing simply because it takes time, it's definitely worth it! Get your project wet, pin it to shape on blocking mats, and let it dry. When steaming or misting, you get your project damp *after* it's pinned in place.

Blocking is important! Don't skip it.

TEN

All About Aftercare

Oh my gosh, you've made it. Your sweater is finished, blocked, and looks amazing. Plus, you've learned so much along the way. If you haven't felt that proud moment of putting on your knit, I want you to do that ASAP. Literally right now. Go to the mirror and check it out at this very moment. You look unreal.

But . . . what's next?

Now comes the aftercare. Hand-knit garments are so amazing, and they can last generations if we take care of them in the right way. Since you've spent so much time crafting your garment, it's essential to learn how to care for it now and in the years to come.

STORING YOUR KNITS

Since we want our items to last as long as possible, there are some things we want to account for that will help them become timeless in our wardrobe.

Fold, don't hang—Hand-knits are quite susceptible to gravity and very prone to stretching. If you can, neatly fold your items and keep them flat, like on a shelf or in a drawer. Not only does this combat the warping of shoulders on hangers, but it also keeps sweaters free from dust and stretching.

Bugs—Depending on where you live in the world, you may need to work against critters, especially moths that might want to take a nibble at those delectable fibers you've chosen. Things such as cedar wood chips, lavender, and citronella oils act as deterrents for moths and bugs. Just remember to replace them each year.

Storing during the offseason—When not wearing your garments for long periods of time, placing your folded pieces in plastic bins or resealable bags is a great way to store your knits. This helps stave off bugs or pests, as well as keep sweaters in a safe environment, such as away from things that may snag them. Note that you must make sure your pieces are 100% dry before putting them away to make sure they don't grow mold.

WASHING

Fact: Hand-knits don't need to be washed as often as you might think. Most knitters and crocheters, on average, will wash their items only once or twice a season: once during the season and again before they put them away in storage until the next year. The interesting thing about wool is that it actually doesn't absorb odors or dirt as much as other fibers. We also tend to wear layers underneath our knits, which helps with the longevity

Note I do not suggest using a dryer at all unless your garment is made of superwash wool, in which case superwash tends to bounce back into shape better with a dryer, but still . . . watch it like a hawk, letting it run for just 5-minute increments.

between washes. That said, if you do want to wash your knits, here are some options.

Spot wash—Dropped some sauce on your sleeve or dribbled some toothpaste on your yoke? A spot wash is your best bet. For smaller spills or anything that may stain if you don't get it off soon, wet the area and rub some gentle detergent/soap on the spot. Rinse and lay flat to dry.

Hand wash—I am a *firm* believer that hand washing is the best way to wash your garments. It's the gentlest on your hand-knits and will keep them in the best shape out of all of these options. To handwash your items, you will essentially repeat the same steps as wet blocking in the previous chapter. I'm a big fan of Eucalan wool wash, as it's a no-rinse detergent that's mild and contains lanolin, which brings back some of the luster to your natural fibers. Once finished, lay your piece out flat to dry. Bonus points: Pin it back into the correct dimensions.

Machine wash—Look at you, living dangerously! Before you even think of machine washing your knits, you'll want to check the washing instructions on the ball band of your yarn. While you *can* machine wash some yarns, most knitters and crocheters opt out, as this is where the most horror stories and mishaps come into play. However, if this is your method of choice and your yarn can withstand it, you'll want to machine wash your sweater or cardi on a delicate cycle and in a delicates' bag, making sure you are not using water that is too hot or too cold. Superwash and acrylic are the most laundry-machine-friendly of yarns, but please still be cautious. Machine washing is the harshest of the washing options and will wear your sweater out more with time. If you do choose to machine wash, make sure to lay the sweater out flat to dry.

Alternative methods—Did you wear your pretty project to a party, and now the lingering scent of someone else's perfume is on it? You have a few options to "air out" your knits without fully washing them. Putting your garment in the freezer, sun-bathing, or snow washing are all options that help combat odors and the growth of bacteria.

Dry cleaning—I wouldn't suggest it. The chemicals used can strip the natural oils from wool and fibers, harming and dulling your garment in the long run. When in doubt, handwash.

DE-PILLING

Depending on the yarn you've used and how often you wear your item, pilling is naturally going to happen as the fibers lift or group together due to the friction of swinging your arms as you walk, putting on your coat, and so on. This is totally normal, and it happens with

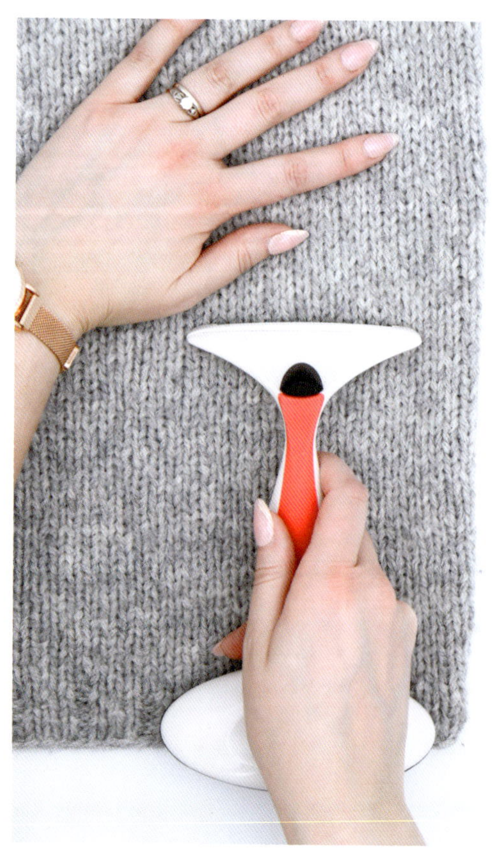

all yarns. Use a gentle de-piller (I like the Gleener, shown here) or your fingers to gently pluck and de-pill the fabric. It's amazing how this one step can bring so much life back into your knit.

MENDING AND REPAIRING

Whether you snag your garment on something or a small (or big!) hole appears in your hand-knit, you can always mend or repair it.

Snags—Using a crochet hook or a darning needle, pull the snagged yarn in reverse to pull the stitch back into place and try your best to even out the surrounding stitches.

Small holes—Using a needle and thread, cinch the hole closed.

Big holes—For larger holes, you might need to darn the hole together. This is a technique where you will weave the thread back and forth across the hole until it's filled in. Google "darning knitwear" for countless video tutorials showing you the process.

FRESHEN THEM UP

Just like humans need to breathe, so do our sweaters, especially if they are knit with natural fibers like wool or camelids. Being in a drawer or in a storage container for a long time can start to stifle your sweaters. These are a few things you can do to freshen them up:

- *Wear them!* We take so much time making these garments, so don't let them sit in a dark corner and never see the light of day!
- Air them out and let in some natural light. Natural fibers tend to get musty, so air them out and give them some indirect sun.
- Take them out of airtight storage bins at least once a season. Shake 'em out.
- Give them a quick steam so you don't have any wrinkles.

TLDR- Too long. Didn't read.

Hand-knit sweaters and cardigans are timeless pieces that can last generations with a few small tips and tricks that help care for them.

While you don't need to wash your item as much as you think, there are a few ways to launder your knits: handwashing, spot washing, and if you're daring enough, machine washing.

When it comes to storing your knits, you will want to neatly fold them and lay them flat instead of hanging them, or they can warp in shape and grow due to gravity. If you plan to put them away in the offseason, you can also fold and place them in airtight containers with items such as cedar chips, citronella, or lavender to ward off bugs and critters.

Other things that you may encounter are pilling, snags, and holes. For de-pilling, an item like a Gleener is helpful. Snags and holes can easily be fixed with some needle and thread—Google "darning" for big holes.

Each of these simple things will help ensure your garments last for as long as possible.

ELEVEN

Sweaters to Knit

Classic Yoke Sweater

The Classic Yoke Sweater is the perfect top-down beginner yoke sweater. Made with an airy size 4 worsted-weight yarn that has the most glorious halo, this design is intended to be worn with 0–5 inches (0–13 cm) of positive ease. With its cozy, chic vibe, slight waist shaping, classic crew neck neckline, and slightly cropped length, it is the quintessential sweater that you'll continue to pull from your closet over and over again. Dress it down with some ripped jeans and sneakers, or pair it with a high-waisted skirt and a French tuck to give it effortless flair. It's up to you!

Knit top-down, in the round, and seamless, this pattern is written in nine sizes—XS (S, M, L, XL) (**2XL, 3XL, 4XL, 5XL**). It is suggested that you highlight all the numbers for your size to avoid confusion. For reference, the model pictured is wearing the size M and is 5 feet 7 inches (1.7 m) tall, 150 pounds (68 kg), and has a bust circumference of 36½ inches (92.5 cm). Please be sure to read through the pattern before proceeding.

Finished Sizes

XS (S, M, L, XL) (**2XL, 3XL, 4XL, 5XL**)
Circumference at bust: 33 (37, 40, 43, 47) (**50, 53, 59, 62**)" / 84 (94, 101.5, 109, 119.5) (**127, 134.5, 150, 157.5**) cm

See the Finished Dimensions table on page 80 for additional measurements.

Yarn

5 (5, 6, 6, 7) (**7, 8, 9, 9**) balls of Lion Brand LB Collection Chainette Yarn or 745 (810, 900, 970, 1,065) (**1,130, 1,200, 1,350, 1,455**) yards / 684 (741, 825, 886, 975) (**1,035, 1,099, 1,235, 1330**) meters size 4 worsted-weight yarn

Needles

- Size U.S. 9 (5.5 mm) set double-pointed needles
- Size U.S. 9 (5.5 mm) 16" (40 cm) circular needles
- Size U.S. 9 (5.5 mm) 24–32" (60–80 cm) circular needles (sizes 2XL and beyond may benefit from a 40" [101 cm] circular needle to accommodate a larger number of stitches)

Adjust needle size as necessary to obtain gauge.

Notions

- Two stitch markers of different colors to identify BOR
- Scissors
- Yarn needle

Gauge

- 16 sts × 21 rounds = 4" (10 cm) in stockinette stitch in the round

Finished Dimensions

Size	Your Bust Circumference	Finished Bust Circumference (A)	Total Length (B)	Length to Underarm (C)	Sleeve Length from CO (D)	Arm Circumference (E)	Wrist Circumference (F)
XS	28–30" (71–76 cm)	33" (84 cm)	21¾" (55 cm)	13½" (34 cm)	24" (61 cm)	13" (33 cm)	7" (18 cm)
S	32–34" (81–86 cm)	37" (94 cm)	22" (56 cm)	13½" (34 cm)	24" (61 cm)	14" (36 cm)	7" (18 cm)
M	36–38" (91–97 cm)	40" (102 cm)	22½" (57 cm)	13½" (34 cm)	24½" (62 cm)	15" (38 cm)	8" (20 cm)
L	40–42" (102–107 cm)	43" (109 cm)	23¼" (59 cm)	13½" (34 cm)	25½" (65 cm)	16" (41 cm)	8" (20 cm)
XL	44–46" (112–117 cm)	47" (119 cm)	23½" (60 cm)	13½" (34 cm)	25½" (65 cm)	16½" (42 cm)	9" (23 cm)
2XL	48–50" (122–127 cm)	50" (127 cm)	24" (61 cm)	13½" (34 cm)	26" (66 cm)	17½" (45 cm)	9" (23 cm)
3XL	52–54" (132–137 cm)	54" (137 cm)	24½" (62 cm)	13½" (34 cm)	26½" (67 cm)	18" (46 cm)	9" (23 cm)
4XL	56–58" (142–147 cm)	59" (150 cm)	25" (63 cm)	13½" (34 cm)	27" (69 cm)	20½" (52 cm)	10" (25 cm)
5XL	60–62" (152–158 cm)	62" (157 cm)	25½" (65 cm)	13½" (34 cm)	28" (71 cm)	21½" (55 cm)	10" (25 cm)

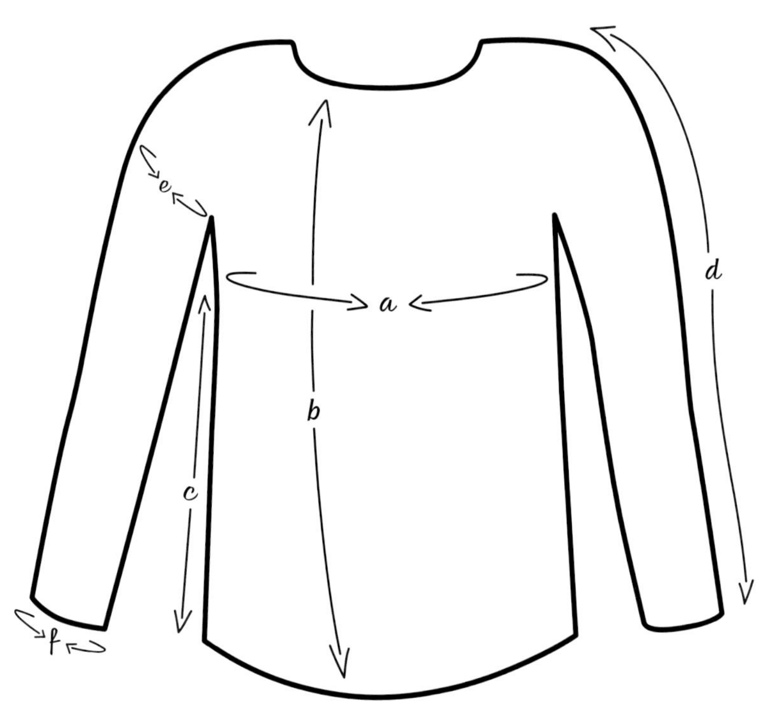

Instructions

COLLAR

On shorter U.S. 9 (5.5 mm) needles, using a long tail cast-on, CO 52 (56, 60, 64, 68) (**72, 76, 80, 84**) sts. Place BOR marker and join in the round.

Rnds 1–6: *K2, P2*.
Rnd 7: K all sts.

BODY

You will now work the body in stockinette stitch in the round with four increase rounds. For all rounds worked without increases, knit all sts. Change from your shorter needle to a longer one when you feel you need more length to accommodate the growing number of stitches.

Increase Rnd 1 (next round): *K1, KFB*. You will have 78 (84, 90, 96, 102) (**108, 114, 120, 126**) sts.

Knit every round until your yoke measures 2 (2, 2¼, 2½, 2½) (**2½, 2¾, 2¾, 3**)" / 5 (5, 5.5, 6.5, 6.5) (**6.5, 7, 7, 7.5**) cm excluding collar.

Increase Rnd 2: *K1, KFB*. You will have 117 (126, 135, 144, 153) (**162, 171, 180, 189**) sts.

Knit every round until your yoke measures 4 (4, 4½, 4¾, 5) (**5, 5½, 5½, 5¾**)" / 10 (10, 11.5, 12, 12.5) (**12.5, 14, 14, 14.5**) cm excluding collar.

Increase Rnd 3: *K2, KFB*. You will have 156 (168, 180, 192, 204) (**216, 228, 240, 252**) sts.

Knit every round until your yoke measures 5¾ (6, 6½, 7, 7¼) (**7½, 8, 8½, 8¾**)" / 14.5 (15, 16.5, 18, 18.5) (**19, 20.5, 21.5, 22**) cm excluding collar.

Increase Rnd 4: *K3, KFB*. You will have 195 (210, 225, 240, 255) (**270, 285, 300, 315**) sts.

Knit every round until your yoke measures 7¾ (8, 8½, 9¼, 9½) (**10, 10½, 11, 11½**)" / 19.5 (20.5, 21.5, 23.5, 24) (**25.5, 26.5, 28, 29**) cm.

In the next round, add 1 (2, 3, 0, 1) (**2, 3, 0, 1**) additional stitches as you see fit around your yoke using a M1R. This

Notes

- When picking your stitch markers before starting the pattern, be sure to have your BOR in a different color to signify the start of the row.
- Change from your shorter needle to a longer one when you feel you need more length to accommodate the growing number of stitches.
- If you find a little gap at the underarms where you picked up stitches, I suggest weaving your ends through those holes to cinch them closed and eliminate any small gaps after completing your piece.

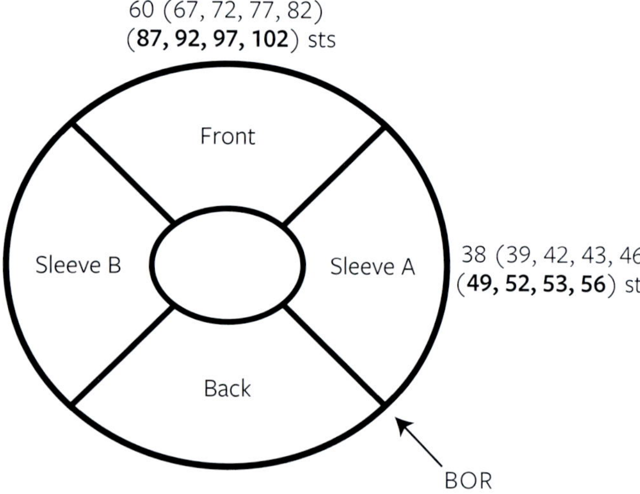

Diagram illustrating your stitch counts before CO under arms. Viewed from the top of your piece.

is done to make your piece divisible by four and evenly split your front, back, and arm sections. You will now have 196 (212, 228, 240, 256) (**272, 288, 300, 316**) sts.

Separate Body and Sleeves

Next, the body and sleeves need to be separated. Your sleeve stitches (Sleeve A and Sleeve B) will be placed on hold with waste yarn (using a darning needle, thread waste yarn through the live sts). The remainder of the body is knit in the round next. Note where your BOR is. You will start here!

Place first 38 (39, 42, 43, 46) (**49, 52, 53, 56**) sts on waste yarn for right sleeve, using backward loop method CO 3 (4, 4, 5, 6) (**7, 7, 11, 11**) sts, place new BOR marker, CO 3 (3, 4, 4, 6) (**6, 7, 10, 11**) sts, K60 (67, 72, 77, 82) (**87, 92, 97, 102**) sts for front, place 38 (39, 42, 43, 46) (**49, 52, 53, 56**) sts on waste yarn for left sleeve, using backward loop method CO 6 (7, 8, 9, 12) (**13, 14, 21, 22**) sts, K all sts until end of round for back. With the sleeves now on hold, you will have 132 (148, 160, 172, 188) (**200, 212, 236, 248**) sts for the body.

BODY

K all sts until the body measures 4" (10 cm) from the underarm.

Waist Shaping

Set-up Rnd: K66 (74, 80, 86, 94) (**100, 106, 118, 124**), PM, K until end of round.

Decrease Rnd: K4, K2tog, K until 6 sts before marker, SSK, K4, SM, K4, K2tog, K until last 6 sts, SSK, K4. (4 sts decreased.)

You now have 128 (144, 156, 168, 184) (196, 208, 232, 244) sts.

K all sts until the body measures 3" (7.5) cm past the decrease round. Repeat the decrease round. You now have 124 (140, 152, 164, 180) (192, 204, 228, 240) sts.

K all sts until the body measures 1" (2.5 cm) past the last decrease round.

Increase Rnd: K4, M1L, K until 4 sts before marker, M1R, M4, SM, K4, M1L, K until last 4 sts, M1R, K4. (4 sts increased.)

K all sts until the body measures 3" (7.5) cm past the increase round. Repeat the increase round. You now have 132 (148, 160, 172, 188) (**200, 212, 236, 248**) sts.

K all sts until the body measures 12" (30.5 cm) from the underarm, or 1½" (4 cm) less than desired finished length. *Note, more rounds will require more yardage.

HEM

Rnds 1–8: *K2, P2.*

Rnd 9: BO all sts in established rib.

Cut your working yarn. We will now move on to the sleeves.

SLEEVES

Transfer held sts from waste yarn onto your U.S. 9 (5.5 mm) double-pointed needles. For sizes 2XL and larger, you're welcome to use the shorter U.S. 9 (5.5 mm) circular if that makes you more comfortable, though you'll need to change to double-pointed needles as you decrease sts.

Set-up Rnd: Starting at the bottom of the armpit (where you backward cast on 6 (7, 8, 9, 12)(**13, 14, 21, 22**) sts for the body) pick up and knit 3 (4, 4, 5, 6) (**7, 7, 11, 11**), place BOR marker, pick up and knit 3 (3, 4, 4, 6) (**6, 6, 10, 11**), K all sleeve sts from on hold. You will have 44 (46, 50, 52, 58) (**62, 66, 74, 78**) sts.

Working your sleeve in the round, K all sts, decreasing every 8 (8, 8, 7, 7) (**6, 5, 4, 4**) rounds.

Example:
Sizes XS–M will work Rnds 1–7 in stockinette (K all sts), decrease on R8.
Sizes L and XL will work Rnds 1–6 in stockinette (K all sts), decrease on R7.

Decrease Rnd: K1, K2tog, K until the last 3 sts, SSK, K1.

Repeat an additional 7 (8, 8, 9, 10) (**12, 14, 16, 18**) times for a total of 8 (9, 9, 10, 11) (**13, 15, 17, 19**) decrease rounds. You will have 28 (28, 32, 32, 36) (**36, 36, 40, 40**) sts and will have worked 64 (72, 72, 70, 77) (**78, 75, 68, 76**) rounds. K all sts until you have worked 102 rounds or until sleeve is 1½" (4 cm) less than desired finished length.

CUFF

Rnds 1–8: *K2, P2*
Rnd 9: BO all sts in 2×2 rib.

Cut working yarn and repeat on the second sleeve.

FINISHING YOUR PIECE

Weave in your ends, block your sweater, and put it on! Do a happy dance because you just finished your #ClassicYokeSweater. You look stunning!

Simple Stockinette Raglan

Ready for your first top-down raglan? Made with a soft acrylic yarn that has the most glorious sheen, the Simple Stockinette Raglan has the signature diagonal line increases, matching double-ribbed collar, sleeves, and hem, and is intended to be worn with ½–3 inches (1.5–7.5 cm) of negative ease. With tailored sleeves and short rows near the underarm separation, this design is meant to fit like a glove and become a staple in your wardrobe.

Knit top-down, in the round, and seamlessly, this pattern is written in nine sizes: XS (S, M, L, XL) (2XL, 3XL, 4XL, 5XL). It is suggested that you highlight all the numbers for your size to avoid confusion. For reference, the model pictured is wearing the size M and is 5 feet 7 inches (1.7 m) tall, 150 pounds (68 kg), and has a bust circumference of 36½ inches (92.5 cm). Please be sure to read through the pattern before proceeding.

Finished Sizes

XS (S, M, L, XL) (**2XL, 3XL, 4XL, 5XL**)
Circumference at bust: 27½ (31½, 36, 39, 43) (**47, 51, 55½, 59**)" / 70 (80, 91.5, 99, 109) (**119.5, 129.5, 141, 150**) cm

See the Finished Dimensions table on page 88 for additional measurements.

Yarn

3 (3, 4, 4, 4) (5, 5, 6, 6) skeins of Lion Brand Heartland or 615 (705, 795, 880, 980) (**1,110, 1,245, 1,365, 1,460**) yards / 560 (645, 725, 800, 895) (**1,015, 1,140, 1,245, 1,335**) meters size 4 worsted-weight yarn

Needles

- Size U.S. 7 (4.5 mm) 16" (40 cm) circular needles
- Size U.S. 7 (4.5 mm) 24–32" (60–80 cm) circular needles (sizes 2XL and beyond may benefit from a 40" [101 cm] circular needle to accommodate a larger number of stitches)
- Size U.S. 6 (4 mm) 16" (40 cm) circular needles
- Size U.S. 6 (4 mm) set double-pointed needles

Adjust needle size as necessary to obtain gauge.

Notions

- Four stitch markers; one should be a different color to identify BOR
- Scissors
- Yarn needle

Gauge

- 16 sts × 22 rows = 4" (10 cm) in stockinette stitch in the round on U.S. 7 (4.5 mm) needles
- 18 sts × 23 rounds = 4" (10 cm) in stockinette stitch in the round on U.S. 6 (4 mm) needles

Finished Dimensions

Size	Your Bust Circumference	Finished Bust Circumference (A)	Total Length (B)	Length to Underarm (C)	Sleeve Length from CO (D)	Arm Circumference (E)	Wrist Circumference (F)
XS	28–30" (71–76 cm)	27½" (70 cm)	23¾" (60.5 cm)	13¾" (35 cm)	18½" (47 cm)	11" (27.5 cm)	8" (20.5 cm)
S	32–34" (81–86 cm)	31½" (80 cm)	24½" (62.5 cm)	13¾" (35 cm)	18½" (47 cm)	11¾" (30 cm)	9" (22.5 cm)
M	36–38" (91–97 cm)	36" (91.5 cm)	25" (63.5 cm)	13¾" (35 cm)	18½" (47 cm)	13" (32.5 cm)	9" (22.5 cm)
L	40–42" (102–107 cm)	39" (99 cm)	25¾" (65 cm)	13¾" (35 cm)	18½" (47 cm)	13¾" (35 cm)	9" (22.5 cm)
XL	44–46" (112–117 cm)	43" (109 cm)	26¼" (67 cm)	13¾" (35 cm)	18½" (47 cm)	15" (38.5 cm)	9" (22.5 cm)
2XL	48–50" (122–127 cm)	47" (119.5 cm)	27½" (69.5 cm)	13¾" (35 cm)	18½" (47 cm)	17" (43 cm)	9¾" (25 cm)
3XL	52–54" (132–137 cm)	51" (129.5 cm)	28½" (72.5 cm)	13¾" (35 cm)	18½" (47 cm)	18½" (46.5 cm	9¾" (25 cm)
4XL	56–58" (142–147 cm)	55½" (141 cm)	29¼" (74.5 cm)	13¾" (35 cm)	18½" (47 cm)	19¾" (50 cm)	9¾" (25 cm)
5XL	60–62" (152–158 cm)	59" (150 cm)	30" (76 cm)	13¾" (35 cm)	18½" (47 cm)	21" (53 cm)	9¾" (25 cm)

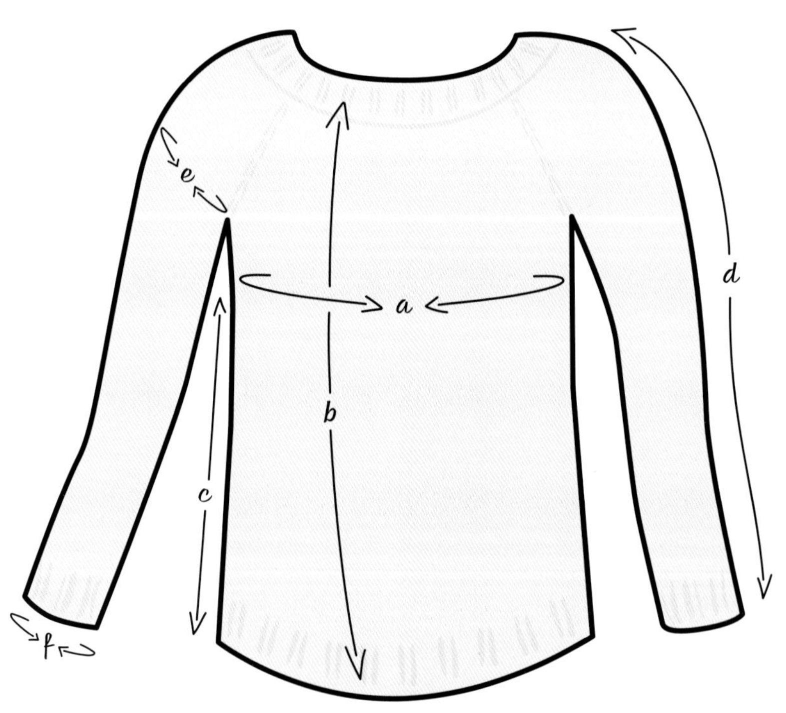

Instructions

COLLAR

On shorter U.S. 7 (4.5 mm) needles, using a long tail cast-on, CO 56 (60, 68, 72, 76) (**80, 84, 88, 88**) sts. Place BOR marker and join in the round.

Rnds 1–6: *K2, P2*.

Set-up Rnd: SM, K11 (10, 10, 10, 10) (**11, 11, 11, 10**), PM, K17 (20, 24, 26, 28) (**29, 31, 33, 34**), PM, K11 (10, 10, 10, 10) (**11, 11, 11, 11**), PM, K17 (20, 24, 26, 28) (**29, 31, 33, 34**) sts.

BEGIN THE RAGLAN

Rnd 1: K all sts.
Rnd 2 (Increase): SM, *K1, KFB, knit to 2 sts before next marker, KFB, K1. Repeat from * until the end of the round. You will have 64 (68, 76, 80, 84) (**88, 92, 96, 96**).

Repeat Rnds 1–2 an additional 18 (20, 21, 23, 25) (**28, 31, 33, 35**) times, for a total of 19 (21, 22, 24, 26) (**29, 32, 34, 36**) times. Change from your shorter needle to a longer one when you feel you need more length to accommodate the growing number of stitches.

You will now have 49 (52, 54, 58, 62) (**69, 75, 79, 82**) sts for right sleeve, 55 (62, 68, 74, 80) (**87, 95, 101, 106**) sts on the front, 49 (52, 54, 58, 62) (**69, 75, 79, 82**) sts for left sleeve, and 55 (62, 68, 74, 80) (**87, 95, 101, 106**) sts on the back for a total of 208 (228, 244, 264, 284) (**312, 340, 360, 376**) sts. Your piece (yoke) should measure 8¼ (9, 9¼, 10, 10¾) (**11¾, 13, 13¾, 14¼**)" / 21 (22.5, 23.5, 25.5, 27) (**30, 33, 34.5, 36.5**) cm from the cast-on edge.

Notes

- When picking your stitch markers before starting the pattern, be sure to have your BOR in a different color to signify the start of the row.
- Change from your shorter needle to a longer one when you feel you need more length to accommodate the growing number of stitches.
- If you find a little gap at the underarms where you picked up stitches, I suggest weaving your ends through those holes to cinch them closed and eliminate any small gaps after completing your piece.

Short-Row Shaping

You will now work short rows into the back of the piece.

Set-up Rnd: K until marker, SM, K until marker, SM, K until marker, SM, K27 (31, 34, 37, 40) (**43, 47, 50, 53**), PM, do not work the rest of this row. You will now work your short rows around this newly placed marker in the center of your back panel.

Short-Row 1: K10 sts past newly placed marker, turn work.
Short-Row 2: MDS, P until marker, SM, P10, turn work.
Short-Row 3: MDS, K until marker, SM, K until 5 sts past last DS (resolving it as you come to it), turn work.
Short-Row 4: MDS, P until marker, SM, P until 5 sts past DS, turn work.

Repeat short rows 3–4 an additional 2 times, for a total of 3 times.

Short-Row 9: MDS, K until end of round, resolving your DS as you come to it.

SEPARATE BODY AND SLEEVES

Next, the body and sleeves need to be separated. Your sleeve stitches (Sleeve A and Sleeve B) will be placed on hold with waste yarn (using a darning needle, thread waste yarn through the live sts). The remainder of the body is knit in the round next. Note where your BOR is. You will start here!

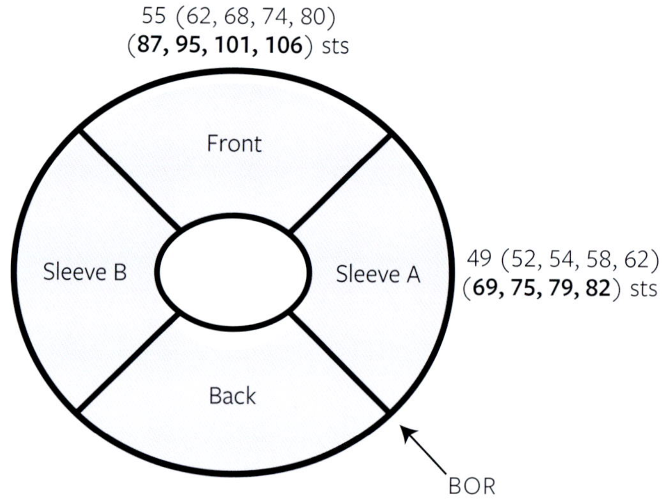

Diagram illustrating your stitch counts before CO under arms. Viewed from the top of your piece.

Place 49 (52, 54, 58, 62) (**69, 75, 79, 82**) sts on waste yarn for right sleeve (these are the stitches from the BOR marker until the next marker), using backward loop method CO 0 (1, 2, 2, 3) (**4, 4, 5, 6**) sts, place new BOR marker, using backward loop method CO 0 (0, 2, 2, 3) (**3, 3, 5, 6**) sts, K all sts to next marker for front, place 49 (52, 54, 58, 62) (**69, 75, 79, 82**) sts onto waste yarn for left sleeve, using backward loop method CO 0 (1, 4, 4, 6) (**7, 7, 10, 12**) sts, K all sts until end of round resolving the remaining DS as you come to it. You can take off the remaining stitch markers as you go. With the sleeves now on hold, you will have 110 (126, 144, 156, 172) (**188, 204, 222, 236**) sts for the body.

BODY

K all sts until 12" (30.5 cm) from the underarm, or 1¾" (4.5 cm) less than desired finished length. *Note, more rounds will require more yardage.

HEM

Set-up Rnd: In the next round sizes XS, S, 4X will need to make the number of stitches divisible by four to match the collar and cuff of the body of the sweater. All other sizes can continue without this step.

Size XS Only

K2tog, K54, K2tog, K until end of round. You have 108 sts.

Size S Only

K2tog, K61, K2tog, K until end of round. You have 122 sts.

Size 4X Only

K2tog, K100, K2tog, K until end of round. You have 200 sts.

ALL SIZES

Rnds 1–10: *K2, P2*.

Rnd 11: BO in established rib.

SLEEVES

Transfer held sts from waste yarn onto your U.S. 6 (4 mm) double-pointed needles. (If you adjusted your needle for gauge, please do the same here.) For sizes 2XL and larger, you're welcome to use the shorter U.S. 6 (4 mm) circular if that makes you more comfortable, though you'll need to change to double-pointed needles as you decrease sts.

Set-up Rnd: Starting at the underarm (where you backward cast on your sts for the body), pick up and knit 0 (0, 2, 2, 3) (**3, 3, 5, 6**) sts, place BOR marker, pick up and knit 0 (1, 2, 2, 3) (**4, 4, 5, 6**) sts, K all sts until end of round. You will now have 49 (53, 58, 62, 68) (**76, 82, 89, 94**) sts.

Working your sleeve in the round, K all sts, decreasing every 9 (9, 6, 6, 5) (**4, 4, 3, 3**) rounds.

Examples:
Sizes XS and S will work Rnds 1–8 in stockinette (K all sts), decrease on R8.
Sizes M and L will work Rnds 1–5 in stockinette (K all sts), decrease on R6.

Decrease Rnd: K1, K2tog, K until the last 3 sts, SSK, K1.

Repeat an additional 5 (5, 8, 10, 13) (**15, 18, 21, 24**) times for a total of 6 (6, 9, 11, 14) (**16, 19, 22, 25**) decrease rounds. You will have 37 (41, 40, 40, 40) (**44, 44, 45, 44**) sts and will have worked 54 (54, 54, 66, 70) (**64, 76, 66, 75**) rounds. K all sts until you have worked 96 rounds or until sleeve is 1¾" (4.5 cm) less than desired finished length.

CUFF

In the next round, sizes XS, S, and 4XL will need to make the number of stitches divisible by four to match the collar and cuff of the body of the sweater. All other sizes can continue without this step.

Sizes XS, S, and 4XL Only
Set-up Rnd: K1, K2tog, K until end of round. You will have 36 (40, -, -, -) (**-, -, 44, -**) sts.

ALL SIZES

Rnds 1–10: *K2, P2*.
Rnd 11: BO in established rib.

Cut working yarn and repeat on the second sleeve.

FINISHING YOUR PIECE

Weave in your ends, block your sweater, and put it on! The #SimpleStockinetteRaglan is done! You look amazing—now twirl, shimmy, or strut, however you like to celebrate.

Neapolitan Pullover

Is anyone craving ice cream suddenly? The Neapolitan Pullover is a seamed drop shoulder sweater made with the coolest yarn. The Bling Bling Yarn is an extremely feathery light yarn that looks like a fingering weight but has a big fluffy halo that makes it an aran-weight #4 yarn. You'll feel like you're wearing a cloud whenever you put it on.

Knit in garter stitch and three colors, this pullover is intended to be worn with 5–7 inches (13–18 cm) of positive ease. Its scoop collar and tapered, extra-long sleeves make this sweater a total go-to in your closet. This pattern is written in nine sizes—XS (S, M, L, XL) (2XL, 3XL, 4XL, 5XL). For reference, the model pictured is wearing the size M and is 5 feet 7 inches (1.7 m) tall, 150 pounds (68 kg), and has a bust circumference of 36½ inches (92.5 cm).

Finished Sizes

XS (S, M, L, XL) (**2XL, 3XL, 4XL, 5XL**)
Circumference at bust: 34 (38, 42, 46, 50) (**54, 58, 62, 66**)" / 86.5 (96.5, 106.5, 117, 127) (**137, 147.5, 158.5, 167.5**) cm

See the Finished Dimensions table on page 96 for additional measurements.

Yarn

- 2 (2, 2, 2, 2) (**2, 3, 3, 3**) balls of We Are Knitters The Bling Bling in Color A (Beige) or 265 (300, 320, 375, 400) (**440, 485, 530, 580**) yds / 242 (275, 295, 345, 365) (**405, 445, 485, 530**) m of size 4 aran weight yarn
- 2 (2, 2, 2, 3) (**3, 3, 3, 3**) balls of We Are Knitters The Bling Bling in Color B (Natural) or 300 (350, 375, 435, 465) (**500, 550, 605, 665**) yds / 375 (320, 345, 400, 425) (**460, 505, 555, 610**) m of size 4 aran weight yarn
- 1 (2, 2, 2, 2) (**2, 2, 3, 3**) balls of We Are Knitters The Bling Bling in Color C (Salmon) or 230 (290, 320, 340, 360) (**400, 440, 465, 490**) yds / 210 (265, 295, 310, 330) (**365, 405, 425, 450**) m of size 4 aran weight yarn

Needles

- Size U.S. 9 (5.5 mm) straight needles or 24–32" (60–80 cm) circular needles
- Size U.S. 9 (5.5 mm) 16" (40 cm) circular needles

Adjust needle size as necessary to obtain gauge.

Notions

- Stitch holder
- Scissors
- Yarn needle

Gauge

- 16 sts × 30 rows = 4" (10 cm) in garter stitch worked flat

Finished Dimensions

Size	Your Bust Circumference	Finished Bust Circumference (A)	Total Length (B)	Length to Underarm (C)	Sleeve Length from CO (D)	Arm Circumference (E)	Wrist Circumference (F)
XS	28–30" (71–76 cm)	35" (89 cm)	17½" (44.5 cm)	7" (18 cm)	20" (51 cm)	14¼" (36 cm)	9" (23 cm)
S	32–34" (81–86 cm)	39" (99 cm)	19¼" (49 cm)	8" (20.5 cm)	20" (51 cm)	16¼" (41.5 cm)	9" (23 cm)
M	36–38" (91–97 cm)	43" (109 cm)	19¼" (49 cm)	8" (20.5 cm)	20" (51 cm)	16¼" (41.5 cm)	9" (23 cm)
L	40–42" (102–107 cm)	47" (119.5 cm)	21" (53.5 cm)	9" (23 cm)	20" (51 cm)	18¼" (46.5 cm)	10" (25.5 cm)
XL	44–46" (112–117 cm)	51" (129.5 cm)	21" (53.5 cm)	9" (23 cm)	20" (51 cm)	18¼" (46.5 cm)	10" (25.5 cm)
2XL	48–50" (122–127 cm)	55" (139.75 cm)	23½" (59.5 cm)	10" (25.5 cm)	20" (51 cm)	20¼" (51.5 cm)	10" (25.5 cm)
3XL	52–54" (132–137 cm)	59" (150 cm)	23½" (59.5 cm)	10" (25.5 cm)	20" (51 cm)	20¼" (51.5 cm)	11" (28 cm)
4XL	56–58" (142–147 cm)	63" (160 cm)	25¼" (64 cm)	11" (28 cm)	20" (51 cm)	22¼" (56.5 cm)	11" (28 cm)
5XL	60–62" (152–158 cm)	67" (170 cm)	25¼" (64 cm)	11" (28 cm)	20" (51 cm)	22¼" (56.5 cm)	11" (28 cm)

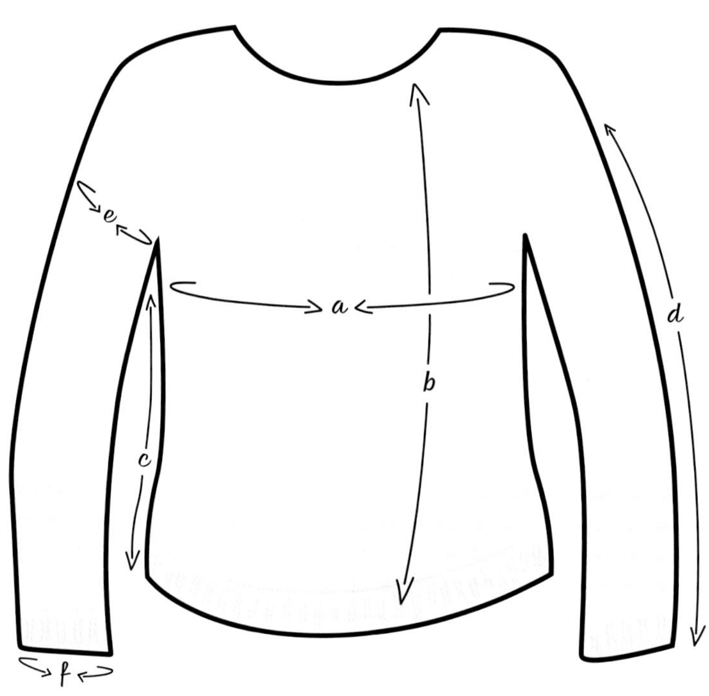

Instructions

FRONT

HEM

Using Color A and US 9 (5.5 mm) needles, CO 70 (78, 86, 94, 102) (**110, 118, 126, 134**) sts.

Working flat:
Rows 1–10: *K1, P1*.

BODY

Continuing in Color A,

Row 1 (RS): K all sts.
Row 2 (WS): K all sts.

Repeat Rows 1–2 (garter stitch) until you have worked 3½ (3¾, 3¾, 4, 4) (**4½, 4½, 4¾, 4¾**)" / 9 (9.5, 9.5, 10, 10) (**11.5, 11.5, 12, 12**) cm in Color A (including the ribbed hem), ending with a WS row.

Notes

- When picking your stitch markers before starting the pattern, be sure to have your BOR in a different color to signify the start of the row.
- Change from your shorter needle to a longer one when you feel you need more length to accommodate the growing number of stitches.
- If you find a little gap at the underarms where you picked up stitches, I suggest weaving your ends through those holes to cinch them closed and eliminate any small gaps after completing your piece.

Cut yarn, switch to Color B.

Repeat Rows 1–2 (Garter stitch) until you have worked 3½ (3¾, 3¾, 4, 4) (**4½, 4½, 4¾, 4¾**)" / 9 (9.5, 9.5, 10, 10) (**11.5, 11.5, 12, 12**) cm in Color B, ending with a WS row.

Cut yarn, switch to Color C.

Repeat Rows 1–2 (garter stitch) until you have worked 3½ (3¾, 3¾, 4, 4) (**4½, 4½, 4¾, 4¾**)" / 9 (9.5, 9.5, 10, 10) (**11.5, 11.5, 12, 12**) cm in Color C, ending with a WS row. Cut yarn.

BEGIN ARMHOLE SHAPING

You will now start shaping the armholes. Be sure to follow the instructions for your size.

Sizes XS–L Only
With Color A,
Row 1 (Decrease): K1, SSK, K until the last 3 sts, K2tog, K1. (2 sts decreased)
Row 2–4: K all sts.

Repeat Rows 1–4 an additional 0 (2, 4, 6, -) (**-, -, -, -**) times for a total of 1 (3, 5, 7, -) (**-, -, -**) times. You will have 68 (72, 76, 80, -) (**-, -, -, -**) sts.

Knit in garter stitch until you have worked 3½ (3¾, 3¾, 4, -) (**-, -, -, -**)" / 9 (9.5, 9.5, 10, -) (**-, -, -, -**) cm in **Color A**.

Cut yarn, switch to Color B.

Knit in garter stitch until you have worked ½ (1¼, 1¼, 2, -) (**-, -, -, -**)" / 1.25 (3, 3, 5, -) (**-, -, -, -**) cm in Color B, ending with a WS row.

Sizes XL–5X Only
With Color A,
Row 1 (Decrease): K1, SSK, K until the last 3 sts, K2tog, K1. (2 sts decreased)
Row 2: K all sts.

Repeat Rows 1–2 an additional - (-, -, -, 9) (**12, 16, 19, 19**) times for a total of - (-, -, -, 10) (**13, 17, 20, 20**) times. You will have - (-, -, -, 82) (**84, 84, 86, 94**) sts.

Knit in garter stitch until you have worked - (-, -, -, 4) (**4½, 4½, 5½, 5½**)" / - (-, -, -, 10) (**11.5, 11.5, 14, 14**) cm in **Color A**. Cut yarn.

Sizes XL-4X Only (Continued)
With Color B, knit in garter stitch until you have worked - (-, -, -, 2) (**2½, 2½, 2½, -**)" / - (-, -, -, 5) (**6.25, 6.25, 6.25, -**) cm in Color B, ending with a WS row.

Size 5X Only (Continued)
You will need to work 4 more decrease rows in Color B.

With Color B, repeat Rows 1–2 an additional—(-, -, -, -) (**-, -, -, 4**) times. You will have—(-, -, -, -) (**-, -, -, 86**) sts.

Knit in garter stitch until you have worked - (-, -, -, -) (**-, -, -, 2½**)" / - (-, -, -, -) (**-, -, -, 6.25**) cm in Color B, ending with a WS row.

ALL SIZES SHAPE NECKLINE

In the next row and continuing with Color B, you will begin shaping the neckline:

Set-up Row (RS): K27 (28, 30, 31, 32) (**33, 33, 33, 33**) and put these stitches on a stitch holder, BO14 (16, 16, 18, 18) (**18, 18, 20, 20**), K until the end of row. You will now work the remaining K27 (28, 30, 31, 32) (**33, 33, 33, 33**) sts for the first shoulder.

Reminder: When binding off in the middle of a round, you must work two new stitches. The stitch left over from your bind-off will join the stitch count in the next panel/group.

First Shoulder
Row 1 (WS): K all sts.
Row 2 (Decrease): K1, SSK, K until the end of row. (1 st decreased)

Repeat Rows 1–2 an additional 5 (5, 5, 5, 5) (**5, 5, 5, 5**) times, for a total of 6 (6, 6, 6, 6) (**6, 6, 6, 6**) times. You will now have 21 (22, 24, 25, 26) (**27, 27, 27, 27**) sts.

Knit in garter stitch until this final **Color B** section measures 3½ (4¼, 4¼, 5, 5) (**5½, 5½, 5½, 5½**)" / 9 (10.75, 10.75, 12.75, 12.75) (**14, 14, 14, 14**) cm.

BO all sts. Leaving a 24" (61 cm) tail, cut your working yarn.

Second Shoulder

Return stitches on hold to needles and join **Color B** at neck edge with WS facing.

Row 1 (WS): K all sts.
Row 2 (Decrease): K until the last 3 sts, K2tog, K1. (1 st decreased)

Repeat Rows 1–2 an additional 5 (5, 5, 5, 5) (**5, 5, 5, 5**) times, for a total of 6 (6, 6, 6, 6) (**6, 6, 6, 6**) times. You will now have 21 (22, 24, 25, 26) (**27, 27, 27, 27**) sts.

Knit in garter stitch until this final Color B section measures 33½ (4¼, 4¼, 5, 5) (**5½, 5½, 5½, 5½**)" / 9 (10.75, 10.75, 12.75, 12.75) (**14, 14, 14, 14**) cm.

BO all sts. Leaving a 4" (10 cm) tail, cut your working yarn.

BACK

Work the same as for the front.

SLEEVES

You will now knit the sleeves from the shoulder to the cuffs, working decreases at the same time that you are changing color from Color B to Color C to Color A, cutting your working yarn after each section. Each color section should be 6¼" (16 cm) long, which is roughly 46 rows.

Using **Color B** and US 9 (5.5 mm) needles, CO 58 (66, 66, 74, 74) (**82, 82, 90, 90**) sts.

Working flat, work in garter stitch (K every row), decreasing every 12 (9, 9, 8, 8) (**6, 6, 5, 5**) rows as follows:

Example:
Size XS will work Rows 1–11 in garter stitch (K all sts), decrease on Row 12.
Sizes S and M will work Rows 1–8 in garter stitch (K all sts), decrease on Row 9.

Decrease Row: K1, K2tog, K the last 3 sts, SSK, K1.

Repeat the decrease row an additional 10 (14, 14, 16, 16) (**20, 19, 23, 23**) times for a total of 11 (15, 15, 17, 17) (**21, 20, 24, 24**) decrease rounds. You will have 36 (36, 36, 40, 40) (**40, 42, 42, 42**) sts and will have worked 132 (135, 135, 136, 136) (**126, 120, 120, 120**) rows.

AT THE SAME TIME, change to Color C when sleeve measures 6¼" (16 cm), and change to Color A when sleeve measures 12½" (31.5 cm).

K in garter stitch until you have worked 138 rows, or until the sleeve is 1½" (4 cm) less than the desired finished length.

CUFF

Continuing in Color A:

Rows 1–8: *K1, P1*.
Row 9: BO all sts in established rib.

ASSEMBLY

At this point I would block all of your pieces before seaming. This will help make seaming a breeze!

Seaming—Shoulders

Place your front and back panels together with RS facing up and shoulders together. Using the horizontal invisible seam technique, sew the shoulder stitches on each side from the armhole edge to the neck edge using the yarn color that will hide the best. Cut working yarn and weave in your ends.

Seaming—Sleeves to Body

Place your body panels RS up on a flat surface. Fold the sleeves in half lengthwise and mark the center of the cast-on edges. Match the center of the cast-on edge of the sleeve to the shoulder seam and use the perpendicular seam technique to sew the sleeves to the body using the yarn color that will hide the best.

Using mattress stitch, sew the sleeve seams, starting at the cuff and moving toward the underarm using the yarn color that will hide the best.

Seaming—Body

Using mattress stitch, Starting at a shoulder seam using color B, sew both side seams on the body, starting at the hem and finishing at the underarm.

Note While working up your sections on the front panel and the first sleeve, make sure to write down how many rows you worked in each section. This way you can do the identical amount on the back panel and second sleeve.

RIBBED COLLAR

Starting at a shoulder seam, using color B and U.S. 9 (5.5 mm) circular needles 16" (40 cm) long, pick up and knit all sts (1 stitch for each garter stitch ridge and 1 stitch for every bound-off stitch around neckline). Adjust if needed so the total is an even number. Place a BOR marker and join to work in the round.

Rnds 1–8: *K1, P1*.
Rnd 9: BO all sts in established rib.

FINISHING YOUR PIECE

Weave in your ends, block your sweater, and put it on! You've completed your #NeapolitanPullover with grace and style. Stunning doesn't even begin to cover it.

Ivy League Vest

Boxy, structured and a mitered collar? Yes, please! This vest knit with size 6 super bulky yarn whips up so fast that you'll feel you've just started and *boom*, you're done. Put it over a collared shirt and wear it to the office or use it as a cozy layer for lounging around the house.

Knit bottom-up and in the round with a drop shoulder, the Ivy League Vest is intended to be worn with 6–8 inches (15–20.5 cm) of positive ease. This pattern is written in nine sizes—XS (S, M, L, XL) (**2XL, 3XL, 4XL, 5XL**). It is suggested that you highlight all the numbers for your size to avoid confusion. For reference, the model pictured is wearing the size M and is 5 feet 7 inches (1.7 m) tall, 150 pounds (68 kg), and has a bust circumference of 36½ inches (92.5 cm). Please be sure to read through the pattern before proceeding.

Finished Sizes

XS (S, M, L, XL) (**2XL, 3XL, 4XL, 5XL**)
Circumference at bust: 36 (40, 44, 48, 52) (**56, 60, 64, 68**)" / 94.5 (101.5, 112, 122, 132) (**142, 152.5, 162.5, 172.5**) cm

See the Finished Dimensions table on page 104 for additional measurements.

Yarn

3 (4, 5, 5) (**6, 6, 7, 7**) balls of Lion Brand Woolease Thick N' Quick or 250 (300, 360, 415, 450) (**495, 545, 600, 660**) yds / 230 (275, 330, 380, 410) (**455, 500, 550, 605**) m of size 6 super bulky yarn

Needles

- Size U.S. 15 (10 mm) 24-32" (60–80 cm) circular needles (sizes 2XL and beyond may benefit from a 40" [101 cm] circular needle to accommodate a larger number of stitches)
- Size U.S. 13 (9 mm) 24-32" (60–80 cm) circular needles (sizes 2XL and beyond may benefit from a 40" [101 cm] circular needle to accommodate a larger number of stitches)
- Size U.S. 13 (9 mm) set double-pointed knitting needles

Adjust needle size as necessary to obtain gauge.

Notions

- Two stitch markers of different colors to identify BOR
- Scissors
- Yarn needle

Gauge

- 8 sts × 12 rounds = 4" (10 cm) in stockinette stitch in the round on U.S. 15 (10 mm) needles

Finished Dimensions

Size	Your Bust Circumference	Finished Bust Circumference (A)	Total Length (B)	Length to Underarm (C)	Armhole Depth (D)
XS	28–30" (71–76 cm)	36" (91.5 cm)	18" (45.5 cm)	9" (23 cm)	9" (23 cm)
S	32–34" (81–86 cm)	40" (101.5 cm)	18¾" (47.5 cm)	9" (23 cm)	9¾" (24.5 cm)
M	36–38" (91–97 cm)	44" (112 cm)	19¼" (49 cm)	9" (23 cm)	10¼" (26 cm)
L	40–42" (102–107 cm)	48" (122 cm)	20½" (52 cm)	9¼" (24 cm)	11" (28 cm)
XL	44–46" (112–117 cm)	52" (132 cm)	20½" (52 cm)	9½" (24 cm)	11" (28 cm)
2XL	48–50" (122–127 cm)	56" (142 cm)	21¾" (55 cm)	10" (25.5 cm)	11¾" (29.5 cm)
3XL	52–54" (132–137 cm)	60" (152.5 cm)	22¼" (56.5 cm)	10" (25.5 cm)	12¼" (31.5 cm)
4XL	56–58" (142–147 cm)	64" (162.5 cm)	23½" (59.5 cm)	10½" (26.5 cm)	13" (33 cm)
5XL	60–62" (152–158 cm)	68" (172.5 cm)	24¼" (61.5 cm)	10½" (26.5 cm)	13¾" (34.5 cm)

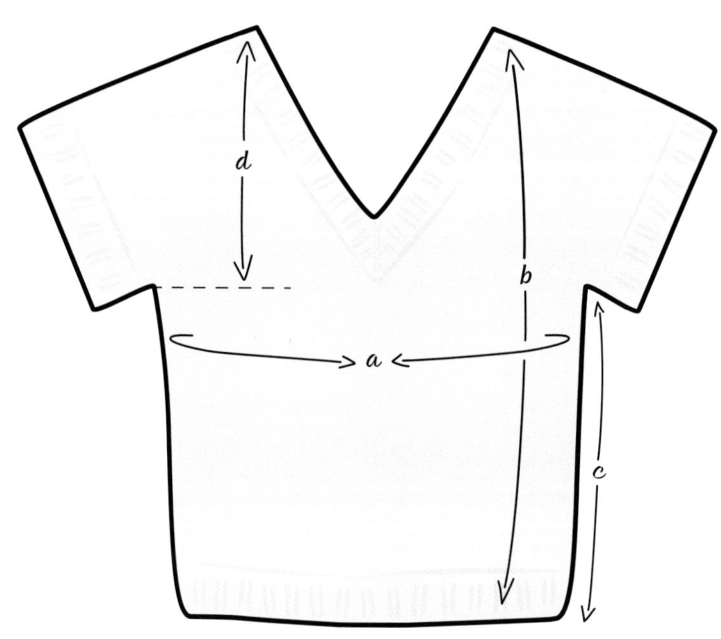

Instructions

HEM

On U.S. 13 (9 mm) needles, using a long tail cast-on, CO 72 (80, 88, 96, 104) (112, 120, 128, 136) sts. Place BOR marker and join in the round.

Rnds 1–6: *K1, P1*.

BODY

Switch to U.S. 15 (10 mm) needles.

Rnd 1: K all sts.

Repeat Rnd 1 until the body measures 9 (9, 9, 9½, 9½) (**10, 10, 10½, 10½**)" / 23 (23, 23, 24, 24) (**25.5, 25.5, 26.5, 26.5**) cm including your ribbed hem.

PANEL SPLIT

You will now separate the body into your front and back panels.

Set-up Row: K37 (40, 44, 47, 51) (**54, 58, 62, 66**), BO 0 (2, 2, 4, 4) (**6, 6, 6, 6**), K35 (37, 41, 43, 47) (**49, 53, 57, 61**), BO 0 (2, 2, 4, 4) (**6, 6, 6, 6**), removing the BOR marker as you come to it. You will now have 37 (39, 43, 45, 49) (**51, 55, 59, 63**) sts in the front and 35 (37, 41, 43, 47) (**49, 53, 57, 61**) sts in the back. You can now place your back panel stitches on hold on scrap yarn.

Reminder: When binding off in the middle of a round, you must work two new stitches. The stitch left over from your bind-off will join the stitch count in the next panel/group.

FRONT PANEL

You will now work the front panel flat.

Row 1: K all sts.
Row 2: P all sts.

Repeat Rows 1–2 an additional 0 (2, 3, 4, 1) (**2, 1, 1, 0**) times, for a total of 1 (3, 4, 5, 2) (**3, 2, 2, 1**) times.

Sizes M and L can now move onto Splitting Your V-Neck.

Sizes XS–S Only

Row 3 (Increase): K1, M1R, K to the last st, M1L K1. (2 sts inc)
Row 4: P all sts.

Repeat Rows 3–4 an additional 1 (0, -, -, -) (**-, -, -, -**) times for a total of 2 (1, -, -, -) (**-, -, -, -**) times. You will have 41 (41, -, -, -) (**-, -, -, -**) sts.

Sizes XL–5X Only

Row 3 (Decrease): K1, SSK, K to the last 3 sts, K2tog, K1. (2 sts dec)
Row 4: P all sts.

Repeat Rows 3–4 an additional - (-, -, -, 1) (**1, 3, 4, 6**) times for a total of - (-, -, -, 2) (**2, 4, 5, 7**) times. You will have - (-, -, -, 45) (**47, 47, 49, 49**) sts.

SPLITTING YOUR V-NECK

Set-up Row: K20 (20, 21, 22, 22) (**22, 23, 24, 24**), knit the next stitch and place it on locking stitch marker before taking it off your needle, K20 (20, 21, 22, 22) (**22, 23, 24, 24**).

You will now work those last K20 (20, 21, 22, 22) (**22, 23, 24, 24**) sts, leaving the first K20 (20, 21, 22, 22) (**22, 23, 24, 24**) sts before the locking stitch marker on hold.

RIGHT NECK

(As if being worn and looking down.)

Starting with a WS row:
Row 1: P all sts.
Row 2 (Decrease): K1, SSK, K to end of row. (1 st decreased)

Repeat Rows 1–2 an additional 9 (9, 10, 10, 11) (**11, 11, 11, 11**) times for a total of 10 (10, 11, 11, 12) (**12, 12, 12, 12**) times. You will have 10 (10, 10, 11, 10) (**11, 11, 12, 12**) sts.

Cut your working yarn, leaving a 36" (91 cm) tail. Place your right front stitches on hold on scrap yarn. You will return to these sts for the three-needle bind-off at the shoulder seam.

LEFT NECK

(As if being worn and looking down.)

Starting with a WS row:
Row 1: P all sts.
Row 2 (Decrease): K to the last 3 sts, K2tog, K1. (1 st decreased)

Repeat Rows 1–2 an additional 9 (9, 10, 10, 11) (**11, 11, 11, 11**) times for a total of 10 (10, 11, 11, 12) (**12, 12, 12, 12**) times. You will have 10 (10, 10, 11, 10) (**11, 11, 12, 12**) sts.

Cut your working yarn, leaving a 36" (91 cm) tail. Place your left front stitches on hold on scrap yarn. You will return to these sts for the three-needle bind-off at the shoulder seam.

BACK PANEL

You will now work the 35 (37, 41, 43, 47) (**49, 53, 57, 61**) sts on the back panel flat. Starting with a RS row and placing the stitches back on your needles:

Sizes XS–L Only

Row 1 (Increase): K1, M1R, K to the last st, M1L, K1. (2 sts increased)

Row 2: P all sts.

Repeat Rows 1–2 an additional 2 (1, 0, 0, -) (**-, -, -, -**) times for a total of 3 (2, 1, 1, -) (**-, -, -, -**) times. You will have 41 (41, 43, 45, -) (**-, -, -, -**) sts.

Sizes XL–5X Only

Row 1 (Decrease): K1, SSK, K to the last 3 sts, K2tog, K1. (2 sts decreased)

Row 2: P all sts.

Repeat Rows 1–2 an additional - (-, -, -, 0) (**0, 2, 3, 5**) times for a total of - (-, -, -, 1) (**1, 3, 4, 6**) times. You will have - (-, -, -, 45) (**47, 47, 49, 49**) sts.

ALL SIZES

Row 3 (RS): K all sts.
Row 4: P all sts.

Repeat Rows 3–4 an additional 10 (12, 14, 15, 15) (**16, 15, 15, 13**) times for a total of 11 (13, 15, 16, 16) (**17, 16, 16, 14**) times.

Row 5: K10 (10, 10, 11, 10) (**11, 11, 12, 12**), BO21 (21, 23, 23, 25) (**25, 25, 25, 25**), K to the end of row. Cut your yarn, leaving a 36" (91 cm) tail.

SEAM YOUR SHOULDERS

Turning your vest inside out, match the tops of the right and left front panels to your back panel. Using the three-needle bind-off, join the shoulders together. Turn your work RS out again to work your ribbed collar.

COLLAR

You will now work the ribbed collar in the round with your U.S. 13 (9 mm) needles. We will be working a mitered ribbing, so we will focus a bit on the stitch in the center of the V-neck.

Starting at the left shoulder seam (as if being worn and looking down), pick up and knit 20 (20, 22, 22, 24) (**24, 24, 24, 24**) sts down the left front neck edge, knit the stitch that is being held by the locking stitch marker (leave the stitch marker in place so you know which stitch is at the center of the mitered corner), pick up and knit 20 (20, 22, 22, 24) (**24, 24, 24, 24**) sts up the right front neck edge to the right shoulder seam, then pick up and knit 21 (21, 23, 23, 25) (**25, 25, 25, 25**) stitches across the bound-off back neck stitches. You will now have 62 (62, 68, 68, 74) (**74, 74, 74, 74**) sts. Place BOR marker and join in the round.

Rnd 1: *K1, P1*.
Rnd 2: *K1, P1; repeat from * to 2 sts before your marked center V-neck stitch, K1, S2KPO, **K1, P1; repeat from ** to end of round.
Rnd 3: *K1, P1; repeat from * to 2 sts before your marked center V-neck stitch, P1, S2KPO, **P1, K1; repeat from ** to the last st, P1.
Rnd 4: Repeat Rnd 2.
Rnd 5: Repeat Rnd 3.
Rnd 6: BO all sts in knit stitches.

Cut yarn and weave in ends.

ARMBANDS

You will now work your armbands in the round, one at a time. Using U.S. 13 (9 mm) double-pointed needles and starting at the bottom of the underarm pick up and knit 36 (42, 44, 48, 48) (**54, 56, 56, 58, 60**) sts evenly around the armhole. Starting at the underarm, pick up and knit 0 (1, 1, 2, 2) (**3, 3, 3, 3**) stitches, place BOR marker, pick up and knit 0 (1, 1, 2, 2) (**3, 3, 3, 3**) stitches, then pick up and knit 1 stitch for every 2 rows along the armhole edge.

Rnds 1–5: *K1, P1*.
Rnd 6: BO all sts in knit stitches.

Cut yarn and weave in ends.

FINISHING YOUR PIECE

Weave in your ends, block your vest, and put it on! You did it! Your #IvyLeagueVest is finished, and you look like a dream. Go ahead, waltz around the living room!

Afternoon Tea Cardi

If you've been looking for a cardigan that will become your go-to, you've just found it. Knit bottom-up, it's got a beautiful drop shoulder construction that drapes especially well over the shoulder due to being knit with a cotton and rayon blend yarn. Pair it with a flowy skirt for an afternoon tea with friends, or with jeans and sneakers, and you've got a total classic on your hands!

With a slight crop, tapered waist, and buttons, the Afternoon Tea Cardi is intended to be worn with 2½–4½ inches (6–11.5 cm) of positive ease at the bust. This pattern is written in nine sizes—XS (S, M, L, XL) (**2XL, 3XL, 4XL, 5XL**). It is suggested that you highlight all the numbers for your size to avoid confusion. For reference, the model pictured is wearing the size M and is 5 feet 7 inches (1.7 m) tall, 150 pounds (68 kg), and has a bust circumference of 36½ inches (92.5 cm). Please be sure to read through the pattern before proceeding.

Finished Sizes

XS (S, M, L, XL) (**2XL, 3XL, 4XL, 5XL**)
Circumference at bust: 33¾ (37¾, 41¾, 45¾, 49¾) (**53¾, 57¾, 61¾, 65¾**)" / 85.5 (95.5, 106, 116, 126) (**136.5, 146.5, 156.5, 167**) cm, buttoned

See the Finished Dimensions table on page 112 for additional measurements.

Yarn

3 (4, 4, 4, 5) (**5, 6, 6, 6**) balls of Lion Brand Coboo or 690 (750, 815, 895, 960) (**1045, 1175, 1260, 1325**) yds / 630 (685, 745, 820, 875) (**955, 1075, 1155, 1210**) m of size 3 DK weight yarn

Needles

- Size U.S. 8 (5 mm) 24–32" (60–80 cm) circular needles (sizes 2XL and beyond may benefit from a 40" [101 cm] circular needle to accommodate a larger number of stitches)
- Size U.S. 8 (5 mm) set double-pointed needles
- Size U.S. 7 (4.5 mm) 24–32" (60–80 cm) circular needles (sizes 2XL and beyond may benefit from a 40" [101 cm] circular needle to accommodate a larger number of stitches)
- Size U.S. 7 (4.5 mm) set double-pointed needles

Adjust needle size as necessary to obtain gauge.

Notions

- Two stitch markers
- Scissors
- Yarn needle
- Three buttons, ¾" (19 mm)

Gauge

- 18 sts × 23 rows = 4" (10 cm) in stockinette stitch worked flat on U.S. 8 (5 mm) needles
- 20 sts × 24 rows = 4" (10 cm) in stockinette stitch in the round on U.S. 8 (5 mm) needles

Finished Dimensions

Size	Your Bust Measurements	Waist Circumference (Buttoned) (A)	Chest Circumference (Buttoned) (B)	Total Length (C)	Length to Underarm (D	Sleeve Length (E)	Upper Arm Circumference (F)	Wrist Circumference (G)
XS	28–30" (71–76 cm)	27½" (69.5 cm)	33¾" (85.5 cm)	18¼" (46 cm)	9¾" (24.5 cm)	18" (45.5 cm)	13½" (34.5 cm)	8½" (21.5 cm)
S	32–34" (81–86 cm)	31½" (80 cm)	37¾" (95.5 cm)	18¼" (46 cm)	9¼" (23.5 cm)	18" (45.5 cm)	14½" (36.5 cm)	8¾" (22.5 cm)
M	36–38" (91–97 cm)	35½" (90 cm)	41¾" (106 cm)	19" (48 cm)	9¼" (24.5 cm)	18" (45.5 cm)	5¼" (38.5 cm)	9¼" (23.5 cm)
L	40–42" (102–107 cm)	39½" (100 cm)	45¾" (116 cm)	19½" (49.5 cm)	9¾" (24.5 cm)	18" (45.5 cm)	16½" (41.5 cm)	9¼" (23.5 cm)
XL	44–46" (112–117 cm)	43½" (110.5 cm)	49¾" (126 cm)	20¼" (51.5 cm)	10" (25.5 cm)	18" (45.5 cm)	16½" (41.5 cm)	9¼" (23.5 cm)
2XL	48–50" (122–127 cm)	47½" (120.5 cm)	53¾" (136.5 cm)	21" (53 cm)	10¼" (26.5 cm)	18" (45.5 cm)	17¼" (43.5 cm)	9½" (24.5 cm)
3XL	52–54" (132–137 cm)	51½" (130.5 cm)	57¾" (146.5 cm)	22¼" (57 cm)	11" (28 cm)	18" (45.5 cm)	18½" (47 cm)	9½" (24.5 cm)
4XL	56–58" (142–147 cm)	55½" (141 cm)	61¾ " (156.5 cm)	22¼" (57 cm)	10¾" (27 cm)	18" (45.5 cm)	19¼" (49 cm)	9½" (24.5 cm)
5XL	60–62" (152–158 cm)	59½" (151 cm)	65¾" (167 cm)	22¼" (57 cm)	11" (28 cm)	18" (45.5 cm)	19¼" (49 cm)	9½" (24.5 cm)

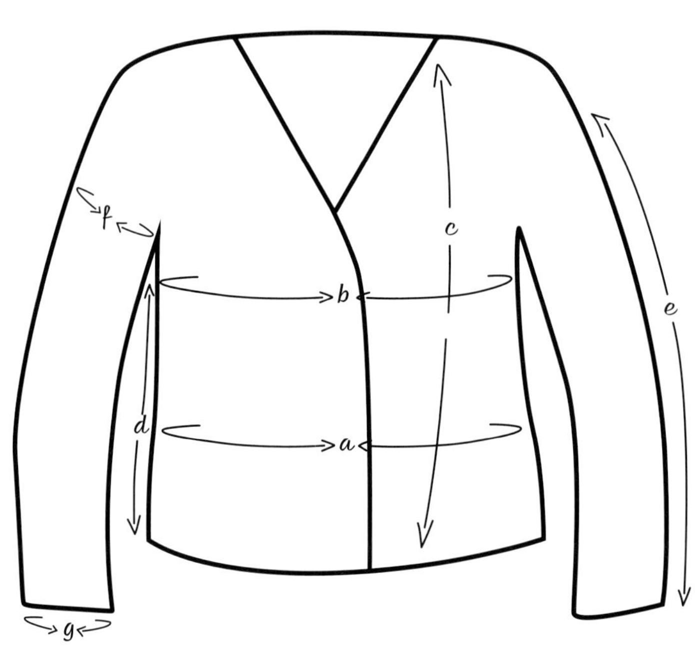

Instructions

HEM

On U.S. 7 (4.5 mm) needles, using a long tail cast-on, CO 118 (136, 154, 172, 190) (208, 226, 244, 262) sts. You will work your piece flat.

Rows 1–12: *K1, P1*.

Note If you're finding a little gap at the underarms where you picked up stitches, I suggest weaving your ends through those holes to cinch them closed and eliminate any small gaps after completing your piece.

BODY

Transfer sts to U.S. 8 (5 mm) needles.

Set-up Row 1 (RS): K29 (34, 38, 43, 47) (**52, 56, 61, 65**), PM, K60 (68, 78, 86, 96) (**104, 114, 122, 132**), PM, K29 (34, 38, 43, 47) (**52, 56, 61, 65**).
Set-up Row 2: P all sts, slipping markers as they come.

Row 1 (Increase): K to 1 st before marker, M1R, K1, SM, K1, M1L, K to 1 st before marker, M1R, K1, SM, K1, M1L, K to end of row. (4 sts increased)
Row 2: P all sts.
Row 3: K all sts.
Row 4: P all sts.
Row 5: K all sts.
Row 6: P all sts.

Repeat Rows 1–6 an additional 5 times, for a total of 6 times. You will have 142 (160, 178, 196, 214) (232, 250, 268, 286) sts.

Row 7 (RS): Repeat Row 1. (4 sts increased)
Row 8: P all sts.
Row 9: K all sts.
Row 10: P all sts.

You will now have 146 (164, 182, 200, 218) (**236, 254, 272, 290**) sts and have worked 54 rows total since cast-on, including your ribbing.

Broken down, you will have 36 (41, 45, 50, 54) (**59, 63, 68, 72**) sts for your front left panel, 74 (82, 92, 100, 110) (**118, 128, 136, 146**) sts for your back panel, and then 36 (41, 45, 50, 54) (**59, 63, 68, 72**) sts for your front right panel.

Sizes S and M can now move onto Division for the Underarms section. All other sizes continue below.

Sizes XS and L–5X Only
Row 11: K all sts.
Row 12: P all sts.

Repeat Rows 11–12 an additional 0 (-, -, 0, 1) (**2, 4, 3, 4**) times for a total of 1 (-, -, 1, 2) (**3, 5, 4, 5**) times. You will have worked 56 (-, -, 56, 58) (**60, 64, 62, 64**) rows. This not only adds length but, combined with the next section, will make your total rows divisible by four, making it easier to pick up stitches for the collar.

DIVISION FOR THE UNDERARMS

After binding off for the underarms, there will be three sections to be worked separately.

Division Row (RS): Removing markers as you go, K34 (39, 43, 47, 51) (**56, 59, 64, 68**), BO4 (4, 4, 6, 6) (**6, 8, 8, 8**), K70 (78, 88, 94, 104) (**112, 120, 128, 138**), BO4 (4, 4, 6, 6) (**6, 8, 8, 8**), K to end of row.

Reminder that when binding off in the middle of the row, the stitch left over from the bind-off will be the first stitch of the next group of knit stitches.

Broken down, you will have 34 (39, 43, 47, 51) (**56, 59, 64, 68**) sts on your LEFT FRONT, 70 (78, 88, 94, 104) (**112, 120, 128, 138**) sts on your BACK PANEL, and 34 (39, 43, 47, 51) (**56, 59, 64, 68**) sts on your RIGHT FRONT. You will now work the last group of 34 (39, 43, 47, 51) (**56, 59, 64, 68**) sts flat for your left front while keeping the rest of the stitches "on hold" on the needles.

LEFT FRONT

(As if looking down and being worn.)

Starting on the WS,
Row 1 (WS): P all sts.
Row 2 (Decrease): K1, SSK, K to the last 3 sts, K2tog, K1. (2 sts decreased; 1 at armhole edge and 1 at neck edge)

Repeat Rows 1–2 an additional 0 (0, 1, 2, 5) (**8, 10, 12, 14**) times for a total of 1 (1, 2, 3, 6) (**9, 11, 13, 15**) times. You will have 32 (37, 39, 41, 39) (**38, 37, 38, 38**) sts.

Row 3 (WS): P all sts.
Row 4 (Decrease): K to the last 3 sts, K2tog, K1. (1 st decreased at neck edge)

Repeat Rows 3–4 an additional 13 (14, 14, 14, 10) (**9, 8, 8, 8**) times for a total of 14 (15, 15, 15, 11) (**10, 9, 9, 9**) times. You will have 18 (22, 24, 26, 28) (**28, 28, 29, 29**) sts.

Row 5 (WS): P all sts.
Row 6: K all sts.

Repeat Rows 5–6 an additional 8 (8, 9, 9, 11) (**10, 11, 10, 7**) times for a total of 9 (9, 10, 10, 12) (**11, 12, 11, 8**) times. You will have worked 48 (50, 54, 56, 58) (**60, 64, 66, 64**) rows since division row.

Row 7 (WS): P all sts.

Leaving a 36" (91 cm) tail, cut working yarn. Leave all sts "on hold" on the needles.

BACK

Join yarn to middle section with the WS facing.

Row 1 (WS): P all sts.
Row 2 (Decrease): K1, SSK, K to the last 3 sts, K2tog, K1. (2 sts decreased)

Repeat Rows 1–2 an additional 0 (0, 2, 3, 6) (**9, 13, 16, 21**) times, for a total of 1 (1, 3, 4, 7) (**10, 14, 17, 22**) times. You will have 68 (76, 82, 86, 90) (**92, 92, 94, 94**) sts.

Row 3 (WS): P all sts.
Row 4: K all sts.

Repeat Rows 3–4 an additional 22 (23, 23, 23, 21) (**19, 17, 15, 9**) times, for a total of 23 (24, 24, 24, 22) (**20, 18, 16, 10**) times. You will have worked 48 (50, 54, 56, 58) (**60, 64, 66, 64**) rows since division row.

Row 5: P18 (22, 24, 26, 28) (**28, 28, 29, 29**), BO32 (32, 34, 34, 34) (**36, 36, 36, 36**), P until end of row.

Leaving a 36" (91 cm) tail, cut working yarn. Leave all sts "on hold" on the needles.

RIGHT FRONT

(As if looking down and being worn.) Join yarn to remaining section with the WS facing.

Row 1 (WS): P all sts.
Row 2 (Decrease): K1, SSK, K to the last 3 sts, K2tog, K1. (2 sts decreased; 1 at armhole edge and 1 at neck edge)

Repeat Rows 1–2 an additional 0 (0, 1, 2, 5) (**8, 10, 12, 14**) times for a total of 1 (1, 2, 3, 6) (**9, 11, 13, 15**) times. You will have 32 (37, 39, 41, 39) (**38, 37, 38, 38**) sts.

Row 3 (WS): P all sts.
Row 4 (Decrease): K1, SSK, K until the end of row. (1 st decreased at neck edge)

Repeat Rows 3–4 an additional 13 (14, 14, 14, 10) (**9, 8, 8, 8**) times for a total of 14 (15, 15, 15, 11) (**10, 9, 9, 9**) times. You will have 18 (22, 24, 26, 28) (**28, 28, 29, 29**) sts.

Row 5 (WS): P all sts.
Row 6: K all sts.

Repeat Rows 5–6 an additional 8 (8, 9, 9, 11) (**10, 11, 10, 7**) times for a total of 9 (9, 10, 10, 12) (**11, 12, 11, 8**) times. You will have worked 48 (50, 54, 56, 58) (**60, 64, 66, 64**) rows since division row.

Row 7: P all sts.
Do not cut your working yarn. You will now use it for the three-needle bind-off.

SEAM YOUR SHOULDERS

Turning the body of your cardigan inside out, match the tops of your front panels to your back panel with the RS together. Using the three-needle bind off, knit together the shoulders.

Turn your work RS out again to begin the sleeves.

SLEEVES

You will now work your sleeves in the round, one at a time. Using U.S. 8 (5 mm) double-pointed needles, with RS facing, and starting at the bound-off edge at the bottom of the underarm, pick up and knit 2 (2, 2, 3, 3) (3, 4, 4, 4), place BOR marker, pick up and knit 2 (2, 2, 3, 3) (3, 4, 4, 4), then pick up and knit 64 (68, 72, 76, 76) (80, 84, 88, 84) sts evenly around remainder of the armhole at the rate of roughly 2 stitches for every 3 rows, for a total of 68 (72, 76, 82, 82) (86, 92, 96, 92) sts.

Working your sleeve in the round, K all sts, decreasing every 6 (6, 6, 5, 5) (**5, 4, 4, 4**) rounds.

Example:
Size XS–M will work Rnds 1–5 in stockinette (K all sts), decrease on Rnd 6.
Sizes L and 2X will work Rnds 1–4 in stockinette (K all sts), decrease on Rnd 5. Sizes 3X-5X will work R1-3 in stockinette (K all sts), decrease on R4.

Decrease Rnd: K1, K2tog, K until the last 3 sts, SSK, K1.

Repeat an additional 12 (13, 14, 17, 17) (**18, 21, 23, 22**) times for a total of 13 (14, 15, 18, 18) (**19, 22, 24, 22**) decrease rounds. You will have 42 (44, 46, 46, 46) (**48,**

48, 48, 48) sts and will have worked 78 (84, 90, 90, 90) (**95, 88, 96, 88**) rounds. K all sts until you have worked 96 rounds or until sleeve is 2" (5 cm) less than desired finished length.

CUFF

Switch to U.S. 7 (4.5 mm) double-pointed needles.

Rnds 1–12: *K1, P1, repeat from * until end of row.
Rnd 13: BO all sts in established rib.

Cut working yarn and repeat for the second sleeve.

COLLAR

Starting at the lower corner of the right front (as if being worn), with the RS facing up, and using your U.S. 7 (4.5 mm) circular needles, pick up and knit 188 (188, 196, 202, 208) (**216, 228, 228, 228**) sts evenly along the front and neck edge at the rate of 3 stitches for every 4 rows along right front edge to the shoulder seam, 1 stitch for every stitch along back neck edge, and 3 stitches for every 4 rows along left front to lower corner.

Set-up Row (WS): *K1, P1*.
Rows 1–4: *K1, P1*.

Buttonholes

Place locking stitch markers to mark the position for three buttonholes along right front edge, with the bottom buttonhole 1" (2.5 cm) above lower edge, the top buttonhole just below the start of the V-neck shaping, and the center buttonhole between these two. Each marker should be placed immediately after a purl stitch. Bonus tip: See how these locking stitch markers land when you are wearing the cardigan. That way you can see if they are sitting where you want them while the item is on.

Row 5, Buttonhole Row (RS): Work in established ribbing to 2 sts before first marker, K2tog, YO, * work in established ribbing to 2 sts before next marker, K2tog, YO, repeat from * one more time, work in established ribbing to end of row. Remove locking stitch markers.

Rows 6–10: *K1, P1*.
Row 11: Loosely BO in established rib.

FINISHING YOUR PIECE

Weave in your ends, sew your buttons on corresponding to your buttonholes, block your sweater, and put it on! You've finished your #AfternoonTeaCardi—and it looks incredible on you. Celebrate your stitches!

Everyday Duster

Say hello to the coziest cardigan in your closet. Made with size 5 bulky-weight yarn, the Everyday Duster knits up in no time. This alpaca blend yarn combined with U.S. 10.5 (6.5mm) needles creates the most glorious drape. With its tapered sleeves, thick collar, and long draping length, this cardigan is just screaming to wrap you up on the couch with a cup of tea and a good book.

Knit from the top-down with a raglan yoke, this design is intended to be worn with 8–11 inches (20.5–28 cm) of positive ease. This pattern is written in nine sizes—XS (S, M, L, XL) (**2XL, 3XL, 4XL, 5XL**). It is suggested that you highlight all the numbers for your size to avoid confusion. For reference, the model pictured is wearing the size M and is 5 feet 7 inches (1.7 m) tall, 150 pounds (68 kg), and has a bust circumference of 36½ inches (92.5 cm). Please be sure to read through the pattern before proceeding.

Finished Sizes

XS (S, M, L, XL) (**2XL, 3XL, 4XL, 5XL**)
Circumference at bust, from edge to edge, no overlap of the front bands: 36¼ (39¾, 43¾, 47¼, 51¼) (**55¾, 59¾, 63¼, 67¼**)" / 92 (101, 111, 120, 130) (**141.5, 152, 160.5, 170.5**) cm

See the Finished Dimensions table on page 122 for additional measurements.

Yarn

7 (8, 8, 9, 10) (**11, 12, 13, 14**) balls of We Are Knitters The Meripaca or 975 (1,120, 1,250, 1,405, 1,575) (**1,705, 1,870, 2,025, 2,185**) yards / 890 (1,020, 1,140, 1,285, 1,440) (**1,560, 1,710, 1,850, 1,995**) meters size 5 bulky-weight yarn

Needles

- Size U.S. 10.5 (6.5 mm) 24–32" (60–80 cm) circular needles (sizes 2XL and beyond may benefit from a 40" [101 cm] circular needle to accommodate a larger number of stitches)
- Size U.S. 10 (6 mm) set double-pointed knitting needles
- Size U.S. 10 (6 mm) 40" (100 cm) circular needles

Adjust needle size as necessary to obtain gauge.

Notions

- Four stitch markers
- Scissors
- Yarn needle

Gauge

- 14 sts × 18 rows = 4" (10 cm) in stockinette stitch worked flat on U.S. 10.5 (6.5 mm) needles
- 15 sts × 20 rows = 4" (10 cm) in stockinette stitch in the round on U.S. 10 (6 mm) needles

Finished Dimensions

Size	Your Bust Circumference	Finished Bust Circumference (A)	Total Length (B)	Length to Underarm (C)	Sleeve Length from Underarm (D)	Arm Circumference (E)	Wrist Circumference (F)
XS	28–30" (71–76 cm)	36¼" (92.5 cm)	36¾" (93.5. cm)	29¾" (75.5 cm)	17" (43.5 cm)	10¾" (27 cm)	9" (23 cm)
S	32–34" (81–86 cm)	39¾" (101 cm)	38¼" (97 cm)	29¾" (75.5 cm)	17" (43.5 cm)	12¼" (31 cm)	9½" (24.5 cm)
M	36–38" (91–97 cm)	43¾" (111 cm)	39" (99.5 cm)	29¾" (75.5 cm)	17" (43.5 cm)	13¾" (35 cm)	9½" (24.5 cm)
L	40–42" (102–107 cm)	47¼" (120 cm)	40½" (102.5 cm)	29¾" (75.5 cm)	17" (43.5 cm)	15½" (39.5 cm)	9½" (24.5 cm)
XL	44–46" (112–117 cm)	51¼" (130 cm)	41¼" (105 cm)	29¾" (75.5 cm)	17" (43.5 cm)	17" (43.5 cm)	10¾" (27 cm)
2XL	48–50" (122–127 cm)	55¾" (141.5 cm)	40¾" (104 cm)	29¾" (75.5 cm)	17" (43.5 cm)	18¼" (46 cm)	10¾" (27 cm)
3XL	52–54" (132–137 cm)	59¾" (152 cm)	41¾" (106 cm)	29¾" (75.5 cm)	17" (43.5 cm)	19¾" (50 cm)	11¼" (28.5 cm)
4XL	56–58" (142–147 cm)	63¼" (160.5 cm)	42¼" (107 cm)	29¾" (75.5 cm)	17" (43.5 cm)	21¼" (54 cm)	11¼" (28.5 cm)
5XL	60–62" (152–158 cm)	67¼" (170.5 cm)	43¼" (110.5 cm)	29¾" (75.5 cm)	17" (43.5 cm)	21¾" (55.5 cm)	12¼" (31 cm)

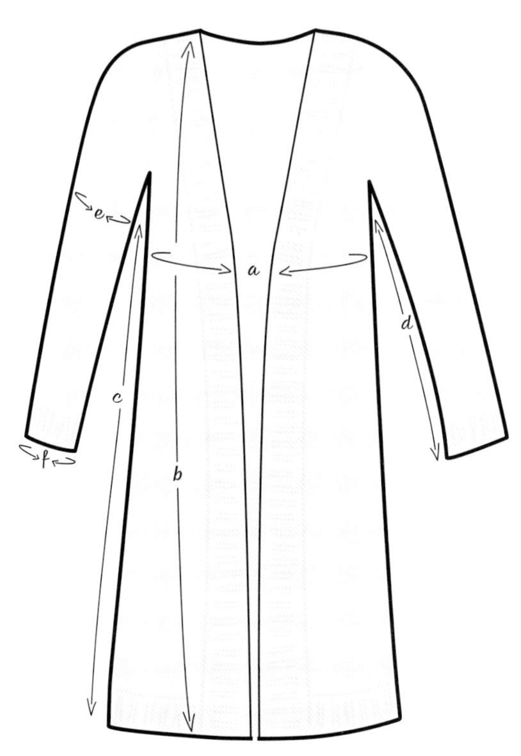

Instructions

START YOKE AND FRONT NECK SHAPING

On U.S. 10.5 (6.5 mm) needles, using the long tail cast-on, CO 36 (36, 40, 40, 44) (44, 48, 48, 52) sts.

Set-up Row 1 (RS): K2 (2, 2, 2, 2) (**2, 2, 2, 2**), PM, K7 (7, 8, 8, 9) (**9, 10, 10, 11**) PM, K18 (18, 20, 20, 22) (**22, 24, 24, 26**) PM, K7 (7, 8, 8, 9) (**9, 10, 10, 11**), PM, K2 (2, 2, 2, 2) (**2, 2, 2, 2**), turn work.
Set-up Row 2 (WS): P all sts.

Row 1 (Increase)(RS): K to 1 st before marker, M1R, K1, SM, K1, M1L, K to 1 st before marker, M1R, K1, SM, K1, M1L, K to 1 st before marker, M1R, K1, SM, K1, M1L, K to 1 st before marker, M1R, K1, SM, K1, M1L, K to end of row. (8 sts increased)
Row 2: P all sts (slipping your markers as you come to them).
Row 3 (Increase): K1, M1R, K to 1 st before marker, M1R, K1, SM, K1, M1L, K to 1 st before marker, M1R, K1, SM, K1, M1L, K to 1 st before marker, M1R, K1, SM, K1, M1L, K to 1 st before marker, M1R, K1, SM, K1, M1L, K to last st, M1L, K1. (10 sts increased)
Row 4: P all sts.

Repeat Rows 1–4 an additional 6 (6, 7, 7, 8) (**8, 9, 9, 10**) times, for a total of 7 (7, 8, 8, 9) (**9, 10, 10, 11**) times. You will have 162 (162, 184, 184, 206) (**206, 228, 228, 250**) sts. You will have 35 (35, 40, 40, 45) (**45, 50, 50, 55**) sts on each sleeve, 46 (46, 52, 52, 58) (**58, 64, 64, 70**) sts on the back, and 23 (23, 26, 26, 29) (**29, 32, 32, 35**) sts on each front panel.

Size 5X Only

Repeat Row 1–2 one more time. You will have 258 sts total; 57 sts on each sleeve, 72 sts on the back and 36 sts on each front panel.

YOKE CONTINUED

Now that the two front panels together have the same number of stitches as the back panel, you will increase at the raglan lines only, without the additional increases at the front edges.

Sizes XS–XL Only

Repeat Rows 1–2 an additional 1 (4, 4, 7, 7) (**-, -, -, -**) times. You will have 170 (194, 216, 240, 262) (**-, -, -, -**) sts. You will have 37 (43, 48, 54, 59) (**-, -, -, -**) sts per sleeve, 48 (54, 60, 66, 72) (**-, -, -, -**) on the back, and 24 (27, 30, 33, 36) (**-, -, -, -**) on each front panel.

So far, you will have worked 32 (38, 42, 48, 52) (**-, -, -, -**) rows.

Note If you're finding a little gap under the arms where you picked up stitches, I suggest weaving your ends through those holes to cinch them closed and eliminate any small gaps after completing your piece.

Sizes 2X–5X Only

Row 5 (RS): K to 1 st before marker, M1R, K1, SM, K1, M1L, K to 1 st before marker, M1R, K1, SM, K1, M1L, K to 1 st before marker, M1R, K1, SM, K1, M1L, K to 1 st before marker, M1R, K1, SM, K1, M1L, K until end of row. (8 sts increased)

Row 6 (WS): P1 to 1 st before marker, M1LP, P1, SM, P1, M1RP, P to 1 st before marker, M1LP, P1, SM, P1, M1RP, P to 1 st before marker, M1LP, P1, SM, P1, M1RP, P to 1 st before marker, M1LP, P1, SM, P1, M1RP, P to end of row. (8 sts increased)

Repeat Rows 5–6 an additional - (-, -, -, -) (**4, 4, 5, 4**) times, for a total of - (-, -, -, -) (**5, 5, 6, 5**) times. You will have- (-, -, -, -) (**286, 308, 324, 338**) sts. You will have - (-, -, -, -) (**65, 70, 74, 77**) sts on each sleeve, - (-, -, -, -) (**78, 84, 88, 92**) sts on the back, and - (-, -, -, -) (**39, 42, 44, 46**) sts on each front panel.

Stop increasing in the arms

Row 7: K to 1 st before marker, M1R, K1, SM, K to marker, SM, K1, M1L, K to 1 st before marker, M1R, K1, SM, K to marker, SM, K1, M1L, K to end of row. (4 sts increased)

Row 8: P1 to 1 st before marker, M1LP, P1, SM, P to marker, SM, P1, M1RP, P to 1 st before marker, M1LP, P1, SM, P to marker, SM, P1, M1RP, P to end of row. (4 sts increased)

Repeat Rows 7–8 an additional - (-, -, -, -) (**0, 0, 0, 1**) times for a total of - (-, -, -, -) (**1, 1, 1, 2**) times. You will have- (-, -, -, -) (**294, 316, 332, 354**) sts. You will have - (-, -, -, -) (**65, 70, 74, 77**) sts on each sleeve, - (-, -, -, -) (**82, 88, 92, 100**) sts on the back, and - (-, -, -, -) (**41, 44, 46, 50**) sts on each front panel.

So far, you will have worked - (-, -, -, -) (**50, 54, 56, 62**) rows since cast-on.

ALL SIZES

Your piece (yoke) should measure 7 (8½, 9¼, 10¾, 11½) (**11, 12, 12½, 13¾**)" / 18 (21.5, 23.5, 27, 29) (**28, 30.5, 32, 35**) cm from the cast-on edge. If you're not yet to these measurements due to a variation in your row gauge, knit every right-side row and purl every WS row until you achieve that length, without working any additional increases. End with a WS row.

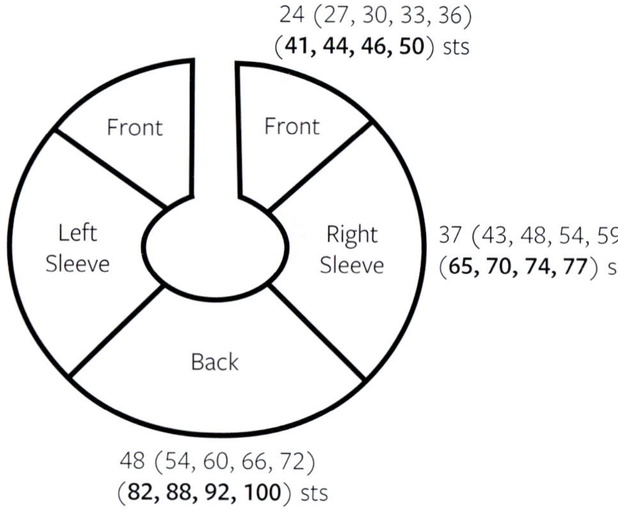

Diagram illustrating your stitch counts before CO under arms. Viewed from the top of your piece.

SEPARATE BODY AND SLEEVES

Next, the body and sleeves need to be separated. Your sleeve stitches will be placed on hold with waste yarn (using a darning needle, thread waste yarn through the live sts). The remainder of the body is knit flat.

Removing the markers as you go, K24 (27, 30, 33, 36) (**41, 44, 46, 50**) sts for left front, place 37 (43, 48, 54, 59) (**65, 70, 74, 77**) sts on waste yarn for left sleeve, using backward loop method CO 3 (3, 4, 4, 5) (**3, 4, 6, 5**) sts, K48 (54, 60, 66, 72) (**82, 88, 92, 100**) sts to next marker for back, place 37 (43, 48, 54, 59) (**65, 70, 74, 77**) sts onto waste yarn for right sleeve, using backward loop method CO 3 (3, 4, 4, 5) (**3, 4, 6, 5**) sts, K24 (27, 30, 33, 36) (**41, 44, 46, 50**) sts to the end of the row for the right front. With the sleeves now on hold, you will have 102 (114, 128, 140, 154) (**170, 184, 196, 210**) sts for the body.

BODY

Set-up Row: P all sts.

Row 1 (RS): K all sts.
Row 2: P all sts.

Repeat Rows 1–2 until your body section (from the yoke separation down) reaches 27" (68.5 cm) and the number of rows (including your yoke rows and the one row worked in the Separate Body and Sleeves plus the set-up row in this section) is divisible by four. This will ensure picking up the stitches for the collar will be easier in the future.

HEM

Rows 1–12: *K1, P1.*
Row 13: BO all sts in established rib.

SLEEVES

Transfer held sts from waste yarn onto your U.S. 10 (6 mm) double-pointed needles. (If you adjusted your needle for gauge, please do the same here.) For sizes XL and larger, you're welcome to use a shorter U.S. 10 (6 mm) circular needle set if that makes you more comfortable, though you'll need to change to double-pointed needles as you decrease sts.

Set-up Rnd: Starting at the underarm (where you backward cast on your sts for the body), pick up and knit 1 (1, 2, 2, 2, 3) (**1, 2, 3, 3**) sts, place BOR marker, pick up and knit 2 (2, 2, 2, 2) (**2, 2, 3, 2**), K all sts from on hold. You will now have 40 (46, 52, 58, 64) (**68, 74, 80, 82**) sts.

Working your sleeve in the round, K all sts decreasing every 24 (14, 9, 6, 6) (**5, 4, 3, 4**) rounds.

Example:
Size S will work Rnds 1–13 in stockinette (K all sts), decrease on Rnd 14.
Sizes L and XL will work Rnds 1–5 in stockinette (K all sts), decrease on Rnd 6.

Decrease Rnd: K1, K2tog, K to the last 3 sts, SSK, K1.

Repeat an additional 2 (4, 7, 10, 11) (**13, 15, 18, 17**) times for a total of 3 (5, 8, 11, 12) (**14, 16, 19, 18**) decrease rounds. You will have 34 (36, 36, 36, 40) (**40, 42, 42, 46**) sts and will have worked 72 (70, 72, 66, 72) (**70, 64, 57, 72**) rounds. K all sts until you have worked 72 rounds or until sleeve is 2" (5 cm) less than desired finished length.

CUFF

Rnds 1–10: *K1, P1.*
Rnd 11: BO all sts in established rib.

Cut yarn and repeat for the second sleeve.

COLLAR

Starting on the bottom right front corner with RS facing you (stockinette facing up) and using your 40" (100 cm) U.S. 10 (6 mm) needles, pick up and knit 3 stitches for every 4 rows along right front edge, 1 stitch for every stitch along cast-on neck edge, and 3 stitches for every 4 rows along left front to bottom corner. The total stitch count should be an even number of stitches.

Row 1: *K1, P1.*

Repeat Row 1 an additional 17 times for a total of 18 times.

Row 2: Loosely BO in established rib.

FINISHING YOUR PIECE

Weave in your ends, block your sweater, and put it on! Do a happy dance because you just finished your #EverydayDuster. You look stunning!

Abbreviations

BO	Bind Off
BOR	Beginning of Round Marker
CO	Cast On
K	Knit
KFB	Knit Front Back
K2tog	Knit 2 Together
M1L	Make 1 Left
M1LP	Make 1 Left Purl
M1R	Make 1 Right
M1RP	Make 1 Right Purl
MDS	Make Double Stitch
P	Purl
PM	Place Marker
RND(S)	Round(s)
RS	Right Side
S2KPO	Slip two, knit two, pass the slipped stitches over
SM	Slip Marker
SSK	Slip-Slip-Knit
St(s)	Stitch(es)
WS	Wrong Side

Special Stitches and Techniques Explained

BINDING OFF

Basic Bind-Off (BO)

Finishing the last row or round of a knitted project so that it will not unravel is called binding off. In the conventional method of binding off, usually done from the right side, you knit the first two stitches, then, using your left needle, lift the second stitch on the right needle up and over the stitch that you've just knit. One stitch is bound off. Repeat this, one stitch at a time, until all stitches are bound off. When a pattern just tells you to bind off all stitches, this is the method to use. If the pattern tells you to bind off in pattern, you knit or purl each stitch following the stitch pattern that has been established before binding it off.

Purl Two Together Bind-Off

You can also bind off from the wrong side, or purl side of stockinette stitching. For this common method of binding off, purl two stitches together (1), transfer this stitch back to your left needle (2), and purl two stitches again (3). Repeat this operation until you've bound off the required number of stitches.

Purl Two Together Bind-Off

1

2

3

1

2

3

Three-Needle Bind-Off

The three-needle bind-off method finishes two edges and joins them together at once. This is especially useful for shoulder seams of sweaters. Both needles must hold the same number of stitches. A third needle is used to bind them off and together.

Hold the two pieces that you're joining with their RS facing each other. Then, insert a third needle knitwise through the first stitch on the front needle and through the first stitch on the back needle (1). Wrap the yarn around the tip of your needle, and pull a loop through both stitches as you simultaneously drop the stitches from the front and back needles (2). Repeat these steps to get a second stitch onto your right needle. Once you have two stitches on your right needle, use the tip of the left needle to lift the second stitch on your right needle up and over the first stitch (3), thus binding off one stitch. Continue in this way to the end of the row.

CASTING ON

Every knitting project begins by putting a foundation row of stitches on your needle; this is called casting on. There are several different ways to cast on stitches. The standard method—the one used if your pattern doesn't specify another method—is called long-tail cast-on.

Long-Tail Cast-On

Make a slipknot on the needle and hold the needle in your right hand. Put the thumb and index finger of your left hand between the tail and working yarn, the tail around your thumb and the working yarn around your index finger. Use the other fingers of your left hand to hold both strands snugly against your left palm (1). Insert the needle upward through the loop on your thumb (2). Pivot the needle to the right and go over and under the yarn on your index finger, picking up a loop (3). Pull the loop back down through the thumb loop (4). Let your thumb drop out of the loop and immediately wrap the tail yarn back around your thumb. Spread your fingers to snug up the new stitch on the needle (5). Repeat the steps for each stitch.

Long-Tail Cast-On

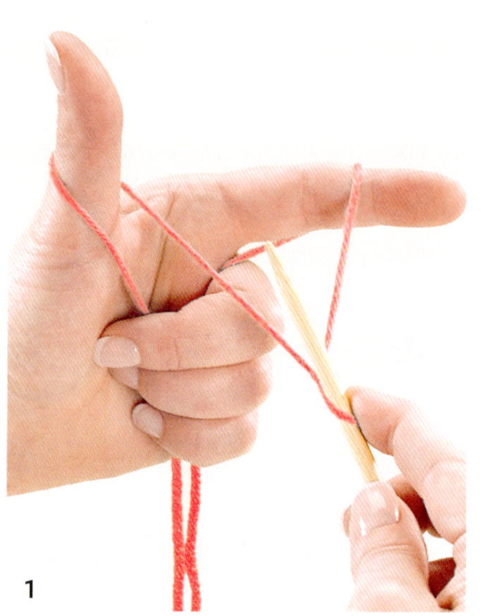
1

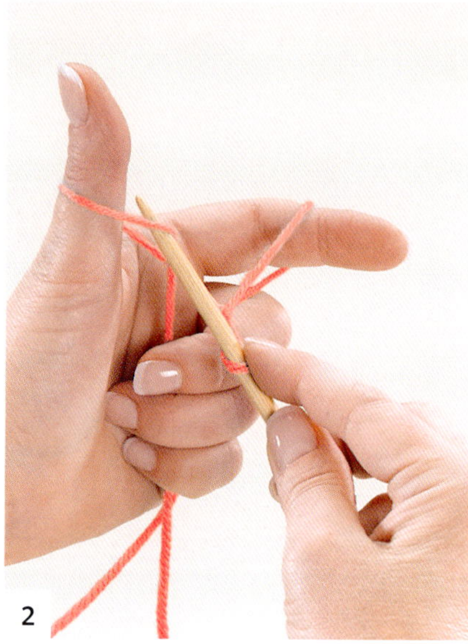
2

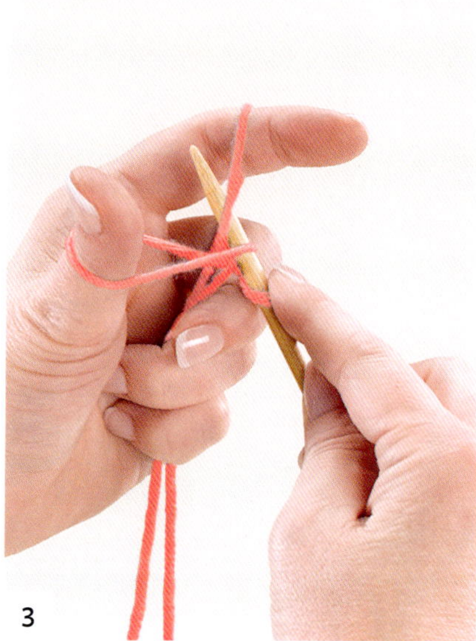
3

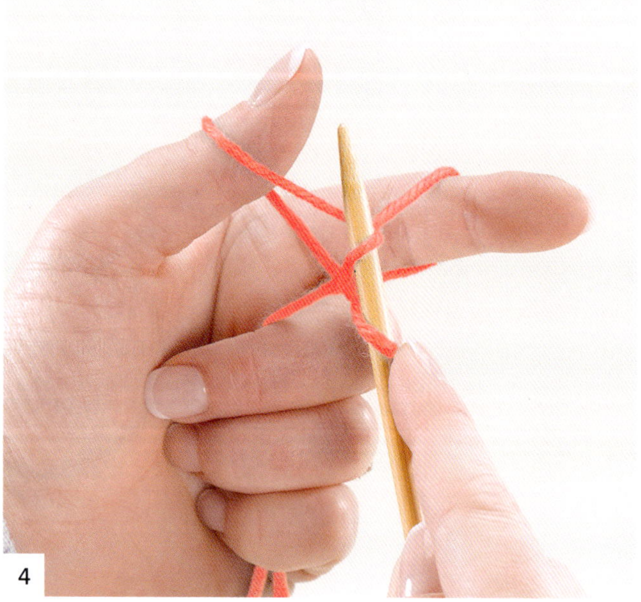
4

5

Cable Cast-On

1

2

3

Knit Two Together (K2tog)

1

2

Cable Cast-On

Other cast-on methods are used in specific situations. The cable cast-on is useful if you need to add stitches to your knitting after you've already worked several rows or rounds, such as underarms.

Insert the right needle into the space between the last two stitches on your left needle. Wrap the yarn around your needle (1) and pull a loop through (2). Put this loop back on your left needle. You've just cast on one stitch. Continue in this manner, adding as many stitches as the pattern calls for (3).

DECREASES

Knit Two Together (K2tog)

Knitting two stitches together has a definite orientation: It is right leaning. The stitch on the left always leans to the right and sits on top of the stitch on the right. Insert the needle knitwise into two stitches together, wrap the yarn around the needle (1), and pull the loop through (2).

Slip-Slip-Knit (SSK)

1

2

Knit Front and Back (KFB)

1

2

3

Slip-Slip-Knit (SSK)

To create a left-leaning decrease that mirrors knitting two stitches together, use a slip-slip-knit. Slip the two stitches knitwise, one at a time (1), and insert your left needle into them to knit them together. You have decreased one stitch, and the right stitch leans on top of the left stitch (2).

S2KPO

Slip 2 stitches together, knit the next stitch, pass the 2 slipped stitches over the stitch just knit. You have 2 stitches decreased.

INCREASES

Knit Front and Back (KFB)

This is one of the simplest increases. Instructions may tell you to knit into the front and back loop of the same stitch. The new stitch that you create with this method will have a little bar at its base, which will be highly visible. Often, the bar increase is used in situations where the bar blends in with the rest of the stitches (as in garter stitch) or when the bar serves a decorative function to highlight the line at which you are increasing stitches.

Knit a stitch, but don't drop it off your left needle (1). Now, insert your right needle into the back loop of the stitch (2), and knit it again, now allowing the stitch to slide off your left needle (3). Your single stitch will now have become two, with the second stitch branching from a little horizontal bar.

Make One Increases (M1L and M1R)

Make one increases are nearly invisible. To perform both the right and the left versions of the make one increase, you pick up the running yarn between your needles, place it on your left needle, and knit into it. How you place the running yarn on your left needle and how you knit into the resulting loop varies, based on whether you are working the right or the left version of the increase.

MAKE ONE RIGHT (M1R)

Unlike decreases, which clearly have a direction in which they slant, increases have a slant that's much more subtle. The right-leaning version of the make one increase, abbreviated M1R, tends to be the default make one increase to use. If the instructions simply say M1, use this method. Insert your right needle under the running yarn from front to back (1). Then, transfer the resulting loop onto your left needle (2). Now, knit into this loop in the normal way, thereby adding an extra stitch to your row (3).

MAKE ONE LEFT (M1L)

To work the left version of the make one increase, insert your left needle under the running yarn from front to back and transfer the loop to your left needle (1). Now, knit into the back loop of this stitch, once again adding an extra stitch to your row.

Make One Increases (M1LP and M1RP)

Make one purl increases are left- and right-leaning increases that are typically done on the wrong side of your piece. When you turn your work to the right side, they should look like an M1L or M1R. For both of these increases, you will knit into the bar/strand that is in between the two stitches.

MAKE ONE RIGHT PURL (M1RP)

With the yarn in the back, insert your left needle and pick up the strand between the two stitches coming from the rear and lift it onto the left needle. This loop should now lean toward the right. Bringing your yarn to

Make One Right (M1R)

1

2

3

Make One Left (M1L)

1

Note the subtle difference in the way these increases slant.

Picking Up Stitches

Stitches picked up along the selvage edge.

the front, insert your right needle purlwise into the front of that extra loop and wrap your yarn counterclockwise. Pull your yarn through and drop it off your left needle, thereby adding an extra stitch to your row.

MAKE ONE LEFT PURL (M1LP)

With the yarn in the back, insert your right needle and pick up the strand between the two stitches coming from the front and lift it onto the left needle. This loop should now lean toward the left. Bringing your yarn to the front, insert your needle into the back loop of that extra loop and wrap your yarn counterclockwise. Pull your yarn through and drop it off your left needle, thereby adding an extra stitch to your row.

PICKING UP STITCHES

Picking up stitches from one edge to begin knitting in a new direction is a common technique used in many types of knitting. When knitting a sweater, for example, you might pick up stitches from the neck opening to add a neck band or collar.

To do this, slip your right needle into an available hole along the indicated edge, wrap your yarn around your needle (1), and pull a loop through onto your right needle (2). Now you've picked up one stitch. Continue in this manner across the edge (or middle) of your work until you've picked up the required number of stitches.

The way you pick up stitches also varies slightly depending on where you are picking up your stitches: from a cast-on or bound-off edge, from a selvage, or from the middle of your fabric.

SEAMING

Mattress Stitch

Mattress stitch is an invisible seaming stitch, useful for attaching two pieces together by their selvages. Lay the pieces edge to edge, right side up. Hook your threaded tapestry needle under the first two running yarns between the selvage and the first column of stitches on one of the pieces. Then, insert your needle under the first two running yarns between the first

Mattress Stitch

1

Horizontal Invisible Hem

1

column of stitches and selvage on the second piece. Zigzag back and forth like this, catching every 2 rows in turn. Leave the stitches fairly loose. After every few stitches, gently pull the yarn to tighten the seam and bring the edges together (1).

Horizontal Invisible Seam

This seam allows you to connect cast-on edges to bound-off edges, cast-on edges to other cast-on edges, and bound-off edges to other bound-off edges. To begin, place the pieces edge to edge, right side up. Hook the needle around the first column of stitches in the first piece, then under the first column of stitches in the second piece (1). Continue in this manner. Note that when you hook the needle under a column of stitches, the column must "point" toward the seam itself. In other words, hook the needle around the base of a knit stitch (bottom of the V) rather than around the top of the knit stitch (the top of the V).

GERMAN SHORT ROWS

German short rows are used to add a wedge of additional fabric to your knitted piece, whether that's at the nape of the neck, the cap of a sleeve, or for horizontal bust darts. When working these short rows, you will work back and forth in rows, even if your project is being knit in the round.

To begin, knit to the turning point and turn the work. Slip the next stitch purlwise (the last stitch worked before you turned). Pull the working yarn up and over the needle to the back until you have created what looks like two stitches. This is making the double stitch (MDS). Continue working the rest of the row as instructed.

To resolve the double stitch, you will knit the double stitch together as one stitch (knitting both little legs you pulled onto the needle). Continue working the pattern as instructed.

Resources

When I started writing the patterns in this book, I wanted to be able to find gorgeous yarns that still felt affordable and didn't leave you staring blank-eyed at the hole in your bank account. Knitting your first sweater is daunting, and it can be even more so when there is an extreme price tag associated with it. Within these pages you will find yarns that range from the super affordable (and available at your local craft store) to a bit more luxurious that you can splurge on while shopping online. I made sure to use a range of fibers and yarn weights, which you learned about in chapter 5: Yarn and Yarn Subbing (p. 39). From wool blends to alpaca to synthetic acrylic to plant-based fibers, the yarns used in each pattern in this book take you through a range of options so you can see what you like best.

Each of these yarns were fantastic to work with, and I want to say thank you again to Lion Brand Yarn and We Are Knitters for supplying the yarn for the patterns in this book!

LION BRAND YARN

www.lionbrand.com

Lion Brand has a soft spot in my heart, as they are the first company that asked me to collaborate with them back in 2017, and since then, I've created 65+ kits with them. So, when this book came around, I knew I wanted to use some of my favorites. And how could I go wrong? A leader in the yarn industry since 1878, Lion Brand has been creating knitter-friendly yarns for more than 140 years.

LB Collection Chainette—#4 medium worsted, currently available in 21 colors

---

My true and ultimate love—this is hands down my most favorite yarn to work with and I hope you get the chance to knit with it as well. If they ever discontinue this yarn, I will throw a temper tantrum. Chainette is a 65% baby alpaca and 35% nylon blend, and its softness is unrivalled. Apt to its name, it's chainette construction, meaning the fibers are formed together to create a hollow and elastic tube that results in the most airy, lightweight yarn that has great stretch. This yarn feels like you're wearing a fingering weight sweater, but works up so quickly as a worsted. It's like wearing a cloud. (The Classic Yoke on page 78 in this book is made of LB Collection Chainette.)

Heartland—#4 medium worsted, currently available in 38 colors

---

If you've got wool allergies or are looking for something to knit up that you can throw in the wash, Lion Brand Heartland is your workhorse. With a bit of a sheen to it, it's 100% acrylic and is super soft on the skin. This yarn is usually my go-to when it comes to baby projects, and with a massive color selection, you can't really go wrong with this size 4 worsted weight yarn. The Simple Stockinette Raglan on page 86 in this book is made out of Lion Brand Heartland.

Wool-Ease Thick & Quick—#6 super bulky, currently available in 79 colors

---

If you're a newbie knitter who lives in Canada or the States, chances are that Lion Brand Thick & Quick was one of your first yarns. This yarn has been a staple in the Knitatude world since I started slangin' knits at markets in 2014, and it still is on my shelves at all times now. With 80% acrylic and 20% wool, it's nice and warm, but doesn't feel overbearing. It lives up to its name as well. Items made with Wool-Ease Thick & Quick are *quick* so don't be surprised when the Ivy League Vest pattern on page 102 in this book is done before you know it.

Coboo—#3 light DK, currently available in 24 colors

Coboo is a lightweight mix of cotton (51%) and bamboo (49%), and is a size 3 DK weight yarn, making it perfect for summertime since its components are plant-based fibers. The yarn is soft to the touch, has cooling properties, and has a slippery feel to it. The drape to Coboo is amazing, and their color selection is *chef's kiss.* The Afternoon Tea Cardi on page 110 in this book is made out of Lion Brand Coboo.

WE ARE KNITTERS

www.weareknitters.com

I also totally have a soft spot for We Are Knitters. Founded in 2011, We Are Knitters has exploded onto the knitting scene and developed a dedicated following of newbie knitters who can't get enough of their yarns. They are the first company that reached out to me for influencer content back in 2015(ish). They sent me the kit for their "Classic Sweater" and it's the first sweater that I actually made myself! Our relationship has only blossomed from there. I knew I had to include them too, so in this book you'll find:

The Bling Bling—#4 medium worsted/aran, currently available in 10 colors

If you love a lil' sparkle in your life, you have just found the perfect yarn. The Bling Bling is the prettiest, most scrumptious wool yarn that has a stunning—but subtle—strand of tinsel in it. It's a bit deceiving as it looks like a fluffy lace-weight mohair, but it's been oomphed up on steroids to make it thicker. It gives the gorgeous airy-type vibe, and you can see that in the Neapolitan Pullover on page 94. Made with 79% Merino (swoon), 3% metallic manufactured fibers (a.k.a. the tinsel) and 18% mohair, this yarn has a beautiful halo to it, and it works up quicker than you would expect.

The Meripaca—#4 medium worsted/aran, currently available in 14 colors

Guh. My second-favorite yarn of all time. This size 4 worsted/aran weight yarn is made of 80% Merino (again, swoon) and 20% alpaca. It's got a bouncy texture that feels silky on the skin, but it's still lightweight and not too dense. Knitting with this in my hands feels like a total delight and I hope you get the chance to use it. However, this yarn tends to lean on the heavier side of worsted, and sometimes you'll even find it in the size 5 bulky/chunky range. It was originally discontinued around 2018, then brought back in 2021. I am hearing rumblings that it might get discontinued before this book releases, and if that's the case I am so sorry. This yarn is truly gorgeous to knit with and that's a tragedy. The Everyday Duster on page 120 is knit with We Are Knitters Meripaca.

Note that yarns come and go, whether a color sells out due to popularity or whether the fiber source discontinues a particular blend. You just can't control what's available when. So, use the skills you learned in chapter 5: Yarn and Yarn Subbing (p. 39) to confidently substitute when needed. There is certainly a lot of yarn out there to choose from!

Acknowledgments

Phew! I can't believe we've come to the end. I want to thank *you*, my beautiful reader. Thank you for trusting me to guide you through making your first garment. I am so deeply honored to have taken any part in your journey, and I'm tickled we could do this together. Thank you for supporting Knitatude, from the bottom of my heart. I wouldn't be here without you.

I want to say that I am a firm believer that you are only as strong as the community that backs you. After writing this book, I can confidently say that I'm lucky to be surrounded by so many incredible people.

To my wonderful husband, Todd . . . I don't even have the words. Thank you for always being my unwavering #1 supporter. For cocking your head when I asked, "Do you think I can write a book?" and responding with an unhesitating "Uh . . . duh." Thank you for raptly listening to me natter on about this book for hours, nodding along as I read out each chapter multiple times and giving me 20-second hugs while I spiraled with self-doubt. Thank you for being kind and compassionate as you tried to read my mind for every "photoshoot Sunday" and for essentially being my hype-man any time I needed it. I love you.

When people ask me where I got my sense of style for my designs and where I got my unnerving discipline for being a hard worker, I always say my mom. I couldn't have gotten through this book without the work ethic you instilled in me. I thought this book was gonna be a cakewalk and holy moly, was I wrong. Thank you for always believing in me and telling me to push for more. I know Dad isn't with us anymore, but I feel he would be quite proud.

When I got the email asking if I wanted to write a book . . . I may have piddled a bit. I want to say thank you to my editor Kerry, who picked me out of the sea of amazing designers and thought I could bring something unique and special to the world. Thank you for believing in me, being honest, keeping me humble, and being a friend throughout this entire process.

To my unreal ladies at Knit Night (special shout out to Nicole, Laura, and Heather), who, without fail, helped me solve problems, gave tips, and became a constant sounding board for any topic that arose for this book. Thank you for keeping me real, making sure I was giving the most accurate info, and even teaching me a few things I didn't know—most of which landed in these very pages.

I want to give a special thanks to my close designer friends, who were always there to lend an ear. Courtney, thank you for always coming off mute during our co-working seshes to answer questions that started with "Now, what if I did . . . " Thank you to Toni, for telling me to advocate for myself, and to Alexi for reminding me that I *do* know what I'm talking about. Thank you to Summer, Angie, Joan, and Janine, for always answering any book-related questions I had. It could be so easy to gatekeep info from each other, but our community constantly proves that wrong.

From taking photos for Knitatude back in 2014 when it all began, all the way to now, working on a book together . . . Kaela, I can't imagine another photographer I would have rather worked with. Thank you for bringing the patterns in this book to life.

About the Author

Thank you to Sandi, for tech editing every pattern and keeping me humble. To my copy editor, Kerri, for making sure my grammar wasn't as bad as Microsoft Word tells me it is. Thank you for every red line, every question, and every "Are you sure about this?" To my testers who gave me their feedback and also helped me ensure these patterns fit as well as I had envisioned, and to everyone else who had a part in making this book come to life: This book wouldn't be what it is without you!

And last but not least, thank you to all my Knitatude fans and followers. I never imagined in 2014 that Knitatude would get to what it is now, let alone having my own book that I can hold in my hands. This glass of champagne? It's to you. *Clink*

Chantal Miyagishima is the purple-haired, potty-mouth knitwear designer and owner behind Knitatude. With a specialty in writing beginner-friendly, size-inclusive patterns that fit, she makes designs that are meant to boost your confidence as you step onto your garment-making journey. If she's not knitting, you can usually find her cuddled up with her two wiener dogs (Kurt Russel and Ashley Spinelli), devouring a romance novel, and being loved on by her husband, Todd. You can find her other designs on Ravelry and Knitatude.ca and can find her on social platforms like Instagram and Facebook through the name Knitatude.

Index